Dark Psychology

Master Persuasion, Negotiation, and NLP and Unlock the Power of Understanding Manipulation, Deception, and Human Behavior

Contents

INTRODUCTION 1

PART 1: THE DARK SIDE 3

CHAPTER 1: DARK PSYCHOLOGY: THE DARK TRIAD 4

ABOUT THE DARK TRIAD 5

HOW TO IDENTIFY DARK TRIAD TRAITS 5

MANAGING PEOPLE WITH DARK TRIAD TRAITS............................. 6

HOW TO COPE WITH ANGER... 7

HOW TO DEAL WITH BULLYING.. 7

SPOTTING A MANIPULATOR 8

DEALING WITH NARCISSISM 8

BUILDING THE SKILLS THAT YOU MAY NEED TO COPE 9

THE IMPACT OF THE DARK TRIAD AT THE WORKPLACE.................... 10

GUARDING YOURSELF AGAINST THE UNDUE INFLUENCE OF DARK
TRIAD INDIVIDUALS 11

CHAPTER 2: THE NINE DARK PERSONALITY TRAITS 13

CHAPTER 3: DARK CRIMINALS AMONG US 16

CRIMINAL MIND VS. CYBERCRIMINAL MIND 18

THE ROLE OF PSYCHOLOGY IN THE LEGAL SYSTEM 18

THE ROLES OF A CRIMINAL PSYCHOLOGIST 19

PROFILING 20

APPLIED CRIMINAL PSYCHOLOGY 22

CHAPTER 4: QUIZ: ARE YOU A DARK PERSONALITY? **24**

INTRODUCTION 24

PART 2: MIND CONTROL, DECEPTION, AND MANIPULATION 29

CHAPTER 5: CREEPY FACTS ABOUT MIND CONTROL **30**

DAILY MIND CONTROL 33

MK-ULTRA 34

ABOUT LSD 35

CHAPTER 6: DECEPTION DETECTION: HOW TO IDENTIFY A LIE **37**

DETECTING DECEPTION 37

HOW TO DETECT AN ANOMALY 37

SIGNS OF DECEPTION 38

CHAPTER 7: WHAT MAKES A CULT? 10 BRAINWASHING TELL-TALE SIGNS **41**

DISINTEGRATING THE CULT PSYCHOLOGY 41

CHAPTER 8: MEDIA MANIPULATION: STRATEGIES AND HOW TO SEE THROUGH THEM **48**

MEDIA MANIPULATION 48

CHAPTER 9: POLITICAL PROPAGANDA: TOOLS, MECHANISMS, AND WAYS TO AVOID IT **52**

TECHNIQUES AND HOW POLITICAL PROPAGANDA WORKS 52

THE TOOLS OF PROPAGANDA 53

LOOKING INTO SOCIAL MEDIA TOOLS 54

CHAPTER 10: PSYCHOLOGICAL WARFARE: DON'T BE MANIPULATED **56**

METHOD 1 – GAINING MANIPULATION SKILLS 56

METHOD 2 – USING DIFFERENT MANIPULATION TECHNIQUES 59

METHOD 3 – MANIPULATE ANYONE IN YOUR LIFE 62

How to Defend Yourself from Manipulative Individuals 66

CHAPTER 11: WORKSPACE MANIPULATORS: SPOT THEM AND STOP THEM 75

Deception Tactics at the Workplace – How to Influence People 75

Which Influence Tactic Is Right for You? 76

Grow Your Core Leadership Skills for Every Role 78

Hack Others' Mind with Cognitive Biases 81

What is the Barnum Effect? 82

How to Use Barnum Statements to Influence People 82

PART 3: UNLOCKING YOUR POWERS 83

CHAPTER 12: NLP: MASTER PERSUASION & NEGOTIATION TECHNIQUES 84

State Control 84

What are the Fundamentals of Human Behavior and Change? 87

How to Safeguard Yourself from Manipulation/Persuasion 88

CHAPTER 13: THE ANTIDOTE TO GROUPTHINK: 10 WAYS TO BEAT THE HERD 93

CHAPTER 14: BODY LANGUAGE: SPEED-READING AND SENDING OUT THE RIGHT MESSAGE 97

Analyzing Different Body Language 100

Watch Out for Yourself and Others 102

CHAPTER 15: CREATING YOUR OWN THOUGHTS 103

Benefits of Creating Your Own Thoughts 105

Tips to Identify That You May Not Be Creating Your Own Thoughts 106

CONCLUSION 107

SOURCES 108

Introduction

The "Dark Triad" personality traits, and they include psychopathy, Machiavellianism, and narcissism. People with some of these traits are fond of manipulating other people that may seem vulnerable to some extent. When a person manipulates another individual, they are focusing on fulfilling their selfish interests. If you are a vulnerable individual, you should focus on learning more about the "Dark Triad" traits.

In this book, you will also learn more about some of the deception tactics used by these individuals. By reading through this dark psychology handbook, you will learn more about the human mind and behavior. Also, you will get to learn more about how people have mastered the art of manipulating their colleagues for their benefit.

By reading through this book, you will also learn more about how you can analyze a person's character and how you can differentiate between the truth and a lie. You will also learn more about how different traits affect the human race. At times, people try to understand others. It may be quite challenging; however, this book will ensure that you have learned more about different issues affecting humanity, including cults and mind control. This handbook will also look at the role of manipulation within the workplace and the family setting. The phenomena refers to how people deceive others, coercing them into doing their bidding. After reading through this book, you will learn more about the traits possessed by malicious individuals. Also, you will learn more about the traits of a person affected by psychopathy, Machiavellianism, and narcissism.

This book will act as your first step to understanding what is required of you when you want to evade people who use manipulation techniques, to stop them from ruining your life. Since the world is turning into a chaotic place, the information in this book will ensure that you can handle different critical issues that may be affecting you as an individual. You can also understand the instances of being abused by close people in your life.

Also, you will learn more about how to defend and safeguard yourself from deception and manipulation. Finally, you will understand more about how to handle vulnerable people effectively in case they need your assistance as a professional. Although many books talk about Dark Psychology, we are happy that you have chosen this specific handbook. I hope that the book is informative, although we have not discussed the entire field of Dark Psychology. We will dig further into the field of Dark Psychology with time. Enjoy your read!

PART 1: The Dark Side

Chapter 1: Dark Psychology: The Dark Triad

People have different personality traits. It is hard to deal with people who are arrogant, volatile, and also domineering. When dealing with certain characters, you should be careful, and you can work on neutralizing their behavior, while also ensuring that you have restored harmony.

There are some characteristics and behaviors that may be seriously damaging, and when a person displays these toxic traits, they may end up undermining their colleagues. Also, some of these traits may end up poisoning and destroying a team. The "Dark Triad" of personality traits comprises of psychopathy, narcissism, and Machiavellianism. In this chapter, the focus will be on these three elements. We will identify all the behaviors associated with each of these elements. Also, we will look at the impact of each of these elements in the workplace.

About the Dark Triad

The "Dark Triad" is not a commonly used phrase in the field of psychology. The term refers to three personality traits, and they may be related to some extent. The personality traits include narcissism, Machiavellianism, and psychopathy.

Narcissism - the term is derived from the Greek myth about the character known as Narcissus; he was a hunter, and he ended up falling in love with his own reflection, while observing himself in a pool of water. He ended up drowning as a result. According to the myth, narcissistic people are normally selfish, arrogant, boastful, and hypersensitive, especially when they are criticized.

Psychopathy - there are different personality traits associated with psychopathy, and they include lack of remorse, lack of empathy, being volatile and manipulative, and antisocial behavior. There is a huge difference between being a psychopath and having psychopathic traits. Psychopathy is normally related to criminal violence.

Machiavellianism - the word is derived from an Italian politician known as Niccolo Machiavelli. He gained a lot of recognition as the author of a book known as *The Prince,* published in 1532. People who have read the book can ascertain that it endorses the dark arts that are associated with deceit and cunning behavior. The traits associated with Machiavellianism include manipulation, duplicity, a lack of morality and emotion, and self-interest.

How to Identify Dark Triad Traits

To identify the Dark Triad traits, psychologists need to measure different personality types. In 2010, Dr. Peter Jonason developed and published a rating scale known as *The Dirty Dozen: A Concise Measure of the Dark Triad* with Gregory Webster, a professional psychologist. The rating scale comprises of a 12-item methodology, and it comes in handy when measuring the dark traits. Psychologists normally ask people to rate themselves using the following questions:

- I tend to lack remorse.
- I have used flattery to get my way.
- I tend to want others to pay attention to me.
- I tend to want others to admire me.
- I tend to exploit others toward my own ends.
- I tend to seek prestige or status.
- I tend to expect special favors from others.
- I tend to be cynical.
- I have used deceit or lied to get my way.
- I tend to manipulate others to get my way.
- I tend not to be too concerned with morality or the morality of my actions.
- I tend to be callous or insensitive.

At a basic level, a person can be rated from one to seven, although the rating scale has twelve questions. The possible score is from 12 to 84. A higher score indicates that a person may possess some of the Dark Triad traits.

Managing People with Dark Triad Traits

If you usually exhibit the Dark Triad traits, you may be wondering whether there is something that you can do about it. The answer to how the Dark Triad traits can be managed is quite complex. Experienced psychologists can weigh into the matter. For starters, when looking into different personality types, you will notice that there are many gradations. A person's behavior can change daily. As a manager, you will have to look into ways that you can address some of the associated negative behaviors so that you can ensure that your team works in harmony, and their productivity levels will also be good.

How to Cope with Anger

There may be some team members who have some psychopathic traits, and they may be prone to aggression and anger. Such situations should be handled quickly. First, make sure that you are conversant with the signs of anger. Normal anger can be spotted easily. For instance, when a person is angry, they may raise their voice, and they may also begin to sweat in the process. Some people try to suppress their anger, and they will showcase some "passive-aggressiveness," and it entails ignoring people, among other things.

Some strategies come in handy when dealing with angry people. If you feel threatened, you should first ensure that you are safe. For instance, you can leave the room instantly. When dealing with a person who has anger issues, you should ensure that you have distanced yourself from these individuals emotionally. Also, make sure that you have identified the cause of the anger. You can become an active listener and also use questioning techniques.

How to Deal with Bullying

At times, anger may roll over to bullying. Bullying is associated with threatening behavior and verbal abuse. It can include unnecessary criticism, spreading some malicious rumors, and belittling someone. It can also be behavior that treats a person as if they are "invisible." If you notice that there is a bully within a specific team, you should start by according the victim some support. Also, you should go ahead and confront the bully while holding them accountable for the damage they have caused.

Spotting a Manipulator

People in the workplace can be influenced in different ways. For instance, you can encourage a person and also praise them depending on the good work that they have done. By inspiring people in the workplace, you will increase the employees' productivity. If one of the team members has some Machiavellian tendencies, they will try to bring about some undue influence on the employees at the workplace by trying to manipulate them. They may also try to coerce the employees through deception.

A manipulative person will always try to hide their behavior, and there are some signs that you should always look out for, such as dealing with a person who cannot take "no" for an answer. Manipulative people will always depict some hurtful behavior when dealing with different people, since they always have some malicious motives.

When you try to challenge a manipulative person, you should be specific about some of the actions that you have spotted. Also, look into how the manipulative person is harming your team. You should go ahead and make it clear to such a person that their behavior cannot be tolerated and that they should change for the better. It is advisable to sign a performance agreement. Such as agreement will ensure that the manipulative person is held accountable in case their actions jeopardize the production levels of the team members.

Dealing with Narcissism

Narcissists are usually selfish, and they can be more of a headache to deal with. They do not pose a major threat; however, when they disrupt the team's morale and harmony, they may fail to realize that they have some undue influence on the team members. It is good to raise such an issue as early as possible after you have realized that there is something wrong.

Narcissists have different character traits, including having a big ego. They can also do anything to gain recognition. They can also demand credit for different ideas that they may have come up with. Despite working with other people as a team, they will go ahead and take credit for the idea as an individual. They also try to dominate meetings and discussions.

A person with a huge ego will not expect to be challenged by another person. When challenging a narcissist, you should make sure that you have stood your ground. You should also arm yourself with some solid counter-arguments. It is also advisable to put a narcissist in a situation whereby they are dependent on the cooperation from other colleagues. By doing so, you will increase the level of understanding and respect among your peers.

Building the Skills that You May Need to Cope

It is not easy to imagine and accept that there exist people with negative behaviors. Also, you may experience some challenges when you are not very confident about winning an argument against another person. There are numerous ways through which you can build on the skills that you need to cope with some of these challenges. For instance, you can learn how to be assertive.

If you have some of these "Dark Triad" personality traits, there are many things that you can do so that you can gain the ability to understand people in a better manner. Also, you can learn more about recognizing a person's emotional perspective and state. You can try to boost your "people skills" by building emotional intelligence and empathy. You should also be aware of people's body language. Additionally, you can manage your emotions using some of these skills. You will also have a greater understanding of how people can help you as you try to spot your patterns comprising of unwanted behavior before you turn into a threat to other team members.

The Impact of the Dark Triad at the Workplace

It is hard to find anything positive relating to the Dark Triad traits, especially at the workplace. People with Dark Triad traits will always display undesirable behavior such as being volatile, aggressive, deceitful, and selfish. Some people may also display a combination of these traits. Various psychologists have been looking into the impact of the Dark Triad. Dr. Seth Spain composed a paper in 2014 named, *The Dark Side of Personality at Work.* In the paper, he stated that there is a relationship between unethical decision-making practices in the workplace and Machiavellianism. Other researchers who have weighed into the matter include Kevin M. Williams and Delroy L. Paulhus, in their 2002 study *The Dark Triad of personality: Narcissism, Machiavellianism, and psychopathy.* Both psychologists argue that some tendencies are associated with Machiavellianism, narcissism, and psychopathy; nevertheless, each of these traits are independent entities. Further research has also been carried out, and there is a huge correlation between lack of humility and dishonesty.

Peter Jonason's 2012 study *The Dark Triad at work : how toxic employees get their way* – with co-authors Sarah Slomski and Jamie Partyka, showcases that employees with Dark Triad traits are usually "toxic" individuals. For instance, the "toxic" employees may bring about some undue influence over other people at the workplace. With time, some of the employees may showcase some aggressiveness, and they may also try to influence people forcefully.

There is evidence that narcissism can be viewed, especially initially, from a positive perspective. In most cases, narcissists make an effort with their appearance and usually are friendly and charming. They will also be achievement-oriented and conscientious, and all these things usually reflect well on an individual. With time, their self-absorbed "me, me, me" attitude may become tiresome.

Guarding Yourself Against the Undue Influence of Dark Triad Individuals

Some psychologists have managed to compose books on how people can safeguard themselves from the undue influence brought about by individuals with Dark Triad traits. According to psychologists such as Oliver James, in his 2013 book *Office Politics: How to Thrive in a World of Lying, Backstabbing and Dirty Tricks,* the Dark Triad tendencies ensure that some employees in the workplace have a nefarious advantage concerning their progression and career growth. When a person is "triadic," they usually exhibit all the traits associated with the Dark Triad, which can help to advance their careers through bullying and manipulating their way up the organization. Some business professionals use the term "think greedy," and the main focus is on attaining their goals regardless of the cost.

Patrick Fagan is an associate lecturer at the University of London, and he has an in-depth understanding of consumer behaviors. According to Patrick Fagan, the Dark Triad traits can help a person to work their way up an organization even if they are unable to get along with other employees. A narcissist will always have high self-esteem, and they may be yearning for the leadership positions within an organization. Psychopathic people will also focus more on being high-achievers, and they will not be concerned about whether their ambitions affect the people around them. As for the Machiavellians, they tend to portray themselves as good people, but are manipulative.

The Dark Triad traits can also bring about "corporate psychopaths," who have a diminished sense of collective responsibility. According to Clive Boddy, a University professor with a doctorate in corporate psychopathy, some of these personality types are common in the finance sector and the civil service.

A person with the Dark Triad traits will always put their needs before those of any other individual within the workplace. The tendencies of people with Dark Triad traits may bring down the organization. If one of the leaders within the organization has showcased Dark Triad traits, the organization cannot easily prosper. If you are a manager, you should always be on the lookout for people with Dark Triad traits. You should deal with such individuals vigorously and guard the other employees against their influence. At times, you may have to remove people from the organization when they exhibit some unwanted characteristics.

Key Points

We had earlier discussed the Dark Triad personality traits, and they include Machiavellianism, Narcissism, and psychopathy. All of these traits are associated with toxicity, and a person with such traits can easily wreak havoc at the workplace. You should always be aware that a person possessing such traits might be a high-achiever, and they may also potentially be charming and achievement-oriented.

Some tools may come in handy when identifying a Dark Triad personality. If you are not a skilled psychologist, you should not attempt to carry out such an assessment individually. If you have noticed some negative behavior from some team members, you should liaise with the human resource manager, and they will look into the matter. Your main responsibility is to ensure that you have managed the impact brought about by the negative behaviors of some employees at the workplace. You should not diagnose any individual in the workplace.

Negative and damaging behaviors should be addressed vigorously and actively. Some of the skills that you may need when dealing with a person with Dark Triad traits include emotional intelligence, assertiveness, and conflict management.

Chapter 2: The Nine Dark Personality Traits

You may know people who are narcissists; however, other character traits may be somewhat intriguing and less well known. According to the study *Measuring the Dark Core of Personality,* by Morten Moshagen, Ingo Zettler, and Benjamin E. Hilbig, (2020), there are nine dark personality traits, and they may be related since they come from a common root. If a person has one of these traits, it is an indicator that they may possess more of the dark personality traits. The study that talked about the nine dark personality traits was published in a peer-reviewed journal. The traits include:

- **Egoism** – this is the preoccupation associated with a person's achievement at the expense of other people.
- **Machiavellianism** – this trait is associated with being manipulative, having a bad attitude, and believing that the end justifies the means.
- **Moral disagreement** – this is the ability to behave in an unethical manner without feeling bad about the outcome.
- **Narcissism** – this trait is associated with superiority, excessive self-absorption, and the extreme need for attention.

- **Psychological entitlement** – this is the belief that you are superior to your counterparts.
- **Psychopathy** – this trait is associated with impulsivity and a lack of empathy.
- **Sadism** – this is the desire to inflict physical or mental harm on other people and also deriving some pleasure from this.
- **Self-interest** – this is the desire to boost your own financial and social status.
- **Spitefulness** – this is a trait associated with the willingness to harm others, and you may also derive some joy from harming yourself.

While studying different individuals, psychologists have been able to identify people with different Dark Triad traits. There was an overlap, and the people who scored a higher rating in one area had a high likelihood of having a higher rating in other areas.

According to the study's authors Moshagen, Zettler, and Hilbig, the root of all these traits is known as the "D-factor," and it can be defined as the "tendency to maximize your utility regardless of the repercussions." The root motivation of people with Dark Triad traits is that they will always put themselves before other people.

For instance, the D-factor is evident in cases of rule-breaking, extreme violence, deception within a company, and lying. If you have learned more about how to assess a person's D-factor, you can easily look into whether a person can engage in different malicious acts.

Different psychologists have written about the D-factor, and it is somewhat similar to the "g" factor of intelligence. According to the g-factor, when a person has a high score in a certain area of intelligence, there is a high likelihood that they will also have a high score in other areas.

In the same way, a high score in one area of the Dark Triad normally goes hand in hand with a high score in other areas. Some of the attempts to explain the Dark Triad traits see them as "indicators" of an adaptive evolutionary strategy that is directed toward gratification and gaining immediate awards. Also, these traits can be associated with reproductive benefits and the survival of a person.

As for the "D-factor," it is quite complicated, and it is more encompassing since it may have other explanations.

What remains to be seen in this case? More research has to be carried out so that we may learn more about the Dark Triad Traits and how they are related, including research focusing more on how each of these traits develop gradually in a person's life. The findings are somewhat intuitive, and studies normally go a long way in showing that all these traits are interconnected, even if we have not gained a full understanding of the interconnection in this case.

Chapter 3: Dark Criminals Among Us

Before a person orchestrates something malicious, they may have thought about everything for a prolonged period, for instance, in the case of a mass shooting. The perpetrator's main motive may be unknown; however, it is evident upon investigation that such people have usually engaged in negative behaviors that are harmful to others close to them.

Some researchers, such as James Alan Fox and Monica J. DeLateur in their paper *Mass Shootings in America: Moving Beyond Newtown* (2013), have looked into the matter, and the difficulty of identifying a potential mass shooter in advance, especially at a tender age. Nevertheless, it is evident that there are some thinking patterns and behaviors that usually manifest with time, and educators also encounter them since they spend a considerable amount of time with pupils. The parents are also familiar with each of these patterns. The main hope is that the children who exhibit each of these traits can outgrow them eventually. Some children do; however, some do not outgrow these traits, and they can harm the people around them. When the patterns intensify, it is important to seek help, and we cannot wait for a seriously malicious action to occur.

When a person engages in crime at a tender age, it is a sign that there is some trouble ahead; not necessarily a mass shooting, however, the behaviors of such people may result in other people being financially, emotionally, and physically hurt.

People with Dark Triad traits may also engage in lying while also blaming other people for their misfortunes. The parents and teachers may not have the ability to control some of the choices that the children make; nevertheless, they may have noticed some warning signs.

Although Dark Triad traits manifest over time, children who simply exhibit some of these traits cannot be labeled as "criminals," since they have not done anything wrong. Since the children are still young, they may still be learning about the world and they can develop more understanding and empathy as they grow. They can turn out as good, well-rounded people, so it is important to support and work with them, without labelling children negatively.

Children are delicate beings, and they should be molded accordingly. When a child is born, people strive to look into whether the child may have learning problems, physical disabilities, and emotional problems. We should also strive to ensure that we have identified other problems that the children may be suffering from so that they cannot injure their peers or cause any harm to themselves, since they do not have any sense of responsibility at a young age, this comes with learning and maturity.

The mental health system should be improved. There should be some strict background checks, and gun laws should also be revised. We should also focus more on identifying some of the "errors" present in the thinking process. We all possess enough knowledge about how we can help children who show potentially harmful traits. The children can be mentored accordingly, and they can hopefully develop more positive traits in the future. Always embark on such a mission with sensitivity and compassion.

Criminal Mind vs. Cybercriminal Mind

In this section, we will look into the cybercriminal mind and the criminal mind. Criminal psychology is also known as criminological psychology, and it is the study of the thoughts, views, actions, and intentions of people that engage in different forms of criminal behavior. The study is related to criminal anthropology, and it delves deep into what drives someone into becoming a criminal. Additionally, the study also looks into a person's reactions after committing a crime.

Criminal psychologists are frequently called up to the stand in court so that they may serve as witnesses, since they have an in-depth understanding of the criminal mind. There are different types of psychiatry, and they also deal with some aspects of criminal behavior. Criminal behavior can be termed as any form of antisocial behavior that is also punishable by the law and the norms within a community. It is, however, somewhat difficult to define the criminal mind.

The Role of Psychology in the Legal System

Psychologists and psychiatrists are normally professionals who are licensed, and they are tasked with assessing the physical and mental state of a person. There are also profilers, and they are tasked with looking for patterns in a person's behavior as they try to identify the person who took part in a certain crime. Some group efforts also focus more on attempting to answer different "common" psychological questions. If a sexual offender is about to commit a re-offending act after being put back into society, how can such an issue be handled? Other issues that arise include; is the sexual offender fit enough to take the stand in court? Was the offender sane when they were committing the offense?

A criminal psychologist may be required to undertake investigative tasks such as examining photographs that were taken at a crime scene. They can also be tasked with interviewing the victim and the suspect. At times, a criminal psychologist comes up with a hypothesis to assess what the offender might do after being released after they have completed their sentence.

The question about a person's competency to stand trial depends on the offender's state of mind as they engaged in the criminal act, and when they are about to take the stand in court. The criminal psychologist will have to assess the ability of the offender to understand the charges that have been placed against them and the possible outcomes that may arise after they are convicted. The offender should also have the ability to offer some assistance to their attorneys as they defend them in court.

The question of criminal responsibility is aimed at assessing the criminal's state of mind as they committed the crime. The main focus is on whether they understand the difference between what is right and wrong and anything that is against the law. The insanity defense is not commonly used, since it cannot be proved easily. If a person succeeds with the insanity defense, they will be sent to a secure hospital facility for a long period as compared to the period that they would have served in prison.

The Roles of a Criminal Psychologist

The roles of a legal psychologist are as follows:

Clinical – In such an instance, the psychologist is supposed to assess an individual so that they can issue a clinical judgment. The psychologist can make use of different assessment tools, psychometric tools, or they can take part in a normal interview with the offender. After that, they are supposed to make an informed decision depending on the outcome of the interview. The assessment comes in handy since it can help the police and other organizations to determine how the offender, in this case, will be processed. For instance, the clinical psychologist can find out whether the offender is sane so that they can stand a trial. They can also determine whether the offender has a mental illness, which relates to whether they are capable of understanding the court proceedings.

Experimental – In this instance, the psychologist is tasked with carrying out some research about the case. They can perform some experiments so that they can illustrate a certain point while also providing further information that will be presented as evidence in court. They may carry out eye-witness credibility and false memory assessments. For instance, they can try to assess whether an eye-witness can spot an object that is 100 meters away.

Advisory – A psychologist is supposed to advise the police about how they should proceed with the investigation. For instance, they can weigh into matters such as which is the best way to interview an eye-witness and the offender. They can also weigh into matters such as how an offender may act after committing a crime.

Actuarial – This is where the psychologist makes use of statistics so that they can inform a case. For instance, they can be tasked with providing the probability of an event taking place. The court may also consider the likelihood of a person engaging in certain acts such as defiling another person sexually after they have served their jail term or after they have been released, if the evidence against them was not strong enough.

Profiling

Criminal profiling is also referred to as offender profiling. It is the process of linking the actions of an offender to the crime scene. The offender's characteristics will also ensure that the police can prioritize and narrow down all possibilities when considering all of the possible suspects. Profiling is quite new concerning forensic psychology. The field of forensic psychology has grown in the past two decades.

Initially, it was an art. Currently, it is a rigorous science. There are different sub-fields in forensic psychology, including investigative psychology. Criminal profiling currently entails carrying out some intensive research and also carrying out some rigorous methodological advances.

Criminals are usually classified based on factors such as sex, age, physical characteristics, geographic region, and education. When comparing some of the similar characteristics, you can easily understand a criminal's motivation when they decide to partake in criminal behavior.

Some national and international security organizations, including the FBI, usually refer to "criminal profiling" as "criminal investigative analysis." The analysts or profilers are normally trained. During the training process, they learn more about the behavioral aspects of different people, and also learn more about the details of unsolved violent crime scenes, whereby there are some traces of psychopathy at the scene where the crime was committed.

A good profiler should be able to deduce the following characteristics after arriving at the crime scene:

1. The amount of planning that went into the crime.
2. The degree of control depicted by the offender.
3. The escalation of emotion at the crime scene.
4. The risk level of the victim and the offender.
5. The general appearance of the crime scene. It may be organized or disorganized.

The profiler can go ahead and interpret the behavior of the offender based on the crime scene. They can discuss everything further with their counterparts.

As a criminal psychologist, you may have to consider profiling from a racial perspective. Race plays a major role in the criminal justice system. In the past few years, the state and federal prisons have held more than 475,900 black inmates. The number of white inmates totaled 436,500. The difference is quite significant. Some of the black people are in prison because of negative stereotypes. Such stereotypes are ineffective, and some criminal psychologists can ascertain that the race of a person does not contribute to them being violent.

There are environmental, cultural, and traditional concepts that surround each race. Each of these concepts plays a key role in psychology. Some people may lack equal opportunities as a result of race or gender, for example, and that means that they have less chances to thrive. Psychologists also try to evaluate whether prison is the most stable place for certain criminals since they may have committed certain offenses as a result of mental illnesses that were not addressed earlier.

Applied Criminal Psychology

For a criminal psychiatrist, the main question is, "Which offender will become a patient?" and "Which patient will become an offender?" Other questions that a psychiatrist should ask themselves is, "Which came first, the mental disorder or the crime?" Psychologists should take a look into the environmental factors and the genetics of a person while they carry out the profiling, to help determine whether the suspect committed the crime or not.

Some of the questions that criminal psychologists should ask themselves include:

- Is the mental disorder present at the moment? Did the person have the mental disorder when they were engaging in the criminal act?

- What is the level of responsibility of the person who committed the crime?

- Is treatment the best option when trying to reduce the risks of reoffending?

- Is there a possibility that the offender may engage in another crime, and what are the risk factors in this case?

The individual psychiatric evaluations normally come in handy since they help to measure an offender's personality traits through psychological testing. The results can also be presented in court.

Chapter 4: Quiz: Are You a Dark Personality?

Some tests have been formulated over the years, and they come in handy when measuring the "Dark Triad" traits.

Introduction

The "Dark Triad" personality traits are three in total. Although each of these traits is independent, they are all closely related, and they may have some malevolent connection. The three traits include Machiavellianism (having a manipulative attitude), psychopathy (lack of empathy), and narcissism (excessive self-love). The Dark Triad is normally assessed depending on each of these mentioned traits. The "Dark Triad" traits can also be tested individually. To measure narcissism, psychologists would make use of the NPI (Narcissistic Personality Inventory). The MACH-IV was used to measure Machiavellianism, and psychopathy was measured using the LSRP (Levenson Self-Report Psychopathy Scale). The differences between each of these tests are present in their analysis aspect. One test that was developed recently includes the *Short Dark Triad (SD3): A Brief*

Measure of Dark Personality Traits, developed by Daniel N. Jones and Delroy L. Paulhus in 2013, and it comes in handy since it produces a uniform assessment.

Procedure

This is a test that is comprised of 26 statements that should be rated depending on how much a person agrees with them. The test should not take a lot of time. It is possible to complete the test in about five minutes.

Participation

This assessment should only be used for educational purposes. The results of the test should not be used when offering psychological advice. If you are interested in learning more about the "Dark Triad" personality traits, and how each trait should be assessed, you should not take this participation test, you should seek advice from a trained professional. This informal test is used for research purposes and should be taken anonymously.

	Disagree	Neutral	Agree
People see me as a natural leader.			
It's not wise to tell your secrets.			
Payback needs to be quick and nasty.			
I avoid dangerous situations.			
I like to use clever manipulation to get my way.			

Many group activities tend to be dull without me.			
It's wise to keep track of information that you can use against people later.			
I insist on getting the respect I deserve.			
I hate being the center of attention.			
There are things you should hide from other people because they don't need to know.			
I like to get revenge on authorities.			
People often say I'm out of control.			
I am an average person.			
Whatever it takes, you must get the important people on your side.			

You should wait for the right time to get back to people.			
I'll say anything to get what I want.			
Make sure your plans benefit you, not others.			
I have never gotten into trouble with the law.			
I know that I am special because everyone keeps telling me so.			
Most people can be manipulated.			
Avoid direct conflict with others because they may be useful in the future.			
People who mess with me always regret it.			
I like to get acquainted with important people.			

I enjoy having sex with people I hardly know.			
I have been compared to famous people.			
It's true that I can be mean to others.			

As per the table above, your answer is graded from 1-3. The results are always issued after you have answered all of the questions in the quiz.

PART 2: Mind Control, Deception, and Manipulation

Chapter 5: Creepy Facts about Mind Control

Mind Control – the term refers to the controversial theory that proposes that it is possible to influence a person's thinking, emotions, behavior, and decisions by outside sources. Mind control is also referred to as "reeducation," "brainwashing," and "coercive persuasion," as well as "brain sweeping," "thought reform" and "thought control."

Creepy Facts about Mind Control

Cults – there are different cults throughout the globe, and they usually focus on brainwashing their followers through mind control. Some well-known cults are self-proclaimed churches and other religious movements. Each cult makes use of different mind control techniques, including isolation and sleep deprivation, in a bid to weaken the mental state of the target, and also to make people susceptible to different religious indoctrinations.

In some cases, the people who have been indoctrinated into one of these churches are first subjected to biblical teachings continuously for about 21 days. The teaching sessions are normally intense, and they usually override a person's ability to view reality as it is, and the cult leaders then take advantage of their followers. The cult leaders succeed in their endeavors by fully overriding a person's thoughts, critical thinking skills, emotions, thoughts, and behavior.

Toxoplasma/Toxoplasmosis – this is a single-celled organism, and there is growing evidence that it can alter a person's behavior. The parasite normally affects living things such as rats, and it can alter their behavior so that they are less risk averse; for example, they can be less afraid of predators like cats. The parasite can also affect humans. When humans consume contaminated meat, soil, or cat poo, they can come become infected with the parasite.

The Devil's Breath – the term was derived from a tree in Colombia known as the Borrachero tree. Scopolamine is thought to affect people who come into contact with it, and they enter into a zombie state when the dust is blown into their faces. The symptoms of the devil's breath include loss of free will, confusion, and memory loss.

When a person is exposed to the devil's breath, they normally become susceptible. Some people claim they have committed crimes while they are under the influence of the devil's breath. When a person engages in a crime under the influence of this drug, they may fail to remember exactly what happened. For instance, an attacker may drug you, and you may end up heeding all their demands. Some attackers may lure you in such a way that you will take them to your home, and they will go ahead and take all the valuables present in the house.

Psychosurgery – this is a controversial means used to treat different psychological disorders. The procedure was administered using a blunt rod through the eye or the temple, and part of the brain tissue would be destroyed. The procedure was commonly referred to as lobotomy, and it was used to treat people who had mental disorders such as schizophrenia. After undergoing the psychosurgery, the patients would become calmer; however, they would exhibit some severe side effects, including memory loss, loss of emotions, child-like behavior, and reduced intellectual functioning. Psychosurgery is still used in the modern era; however, it is used as a last resort.

The Remote-Control Bull – the technique was invented by Dr. Jose Delgado in 1963, and he was able to control bulls using a chip that would be implanted into the brain of the bull. When the bull started to charge, Delgado would use a remote button to stop the bull. The chip would use a "stimoceiver," and it would stimulate some parts of the brain. Some researchers have been looking into the experiments carried out by Dr. Delgado, and they are bound to improve the technology greatly. With time, they can use the technique on animals such as rats, sharks, and pigeons.

Mind-Controlled Delusions – some researchers have been using hypnosis while investigating delusions and psychosis in healthy people. Using hypnosis, a scientist can take control of a person's mind to cause them to hallucinate, while recording the effect of the hypnosis on each patient. While hypnotized, the patients normally have an out of body experience, and they normally feel that they are being manipulated like puppets by a puppeteer.

Hypno-mugging – there are some instances where people have been mugged after being hypnotized. For instance, a thief may act friendly, and after a few minutes, they can put you in a trance. When a robber learns more about hypnosis, they can easily attack different people, and they can frisk them in broad daylight. Hypnosis is not a common technique when it comes to mugging people.

MK-ULTRA – this is the name of a code that refers to different experiments that were carried out by the CIA during the 1950s. The experiments were carried out using different methods such as psychoactive drugs, sensory deprivation, and isolation, and the main focus was on altering a person's brain functions and mental state – the program aimed at creating spies against their own will. The MK-ULTRA program managed to manipulate the mental state of different people.

Subliminal Messages – "subliminal messaging" refers to the ability to pass a message to another person, and they will not be able to recognize the message consciously. There have been some reports that there are some subliminal messages in films and advertisements.

Some music videos also contain subliminal messages. The messages, in this case, may relate to purchasing different products, for example. But these kinds of subconscious messages could potentially have a more sinister effect, depending on the message. Over the years, there have been many debates about subliminal messages.

Ultrasound Soldiers – the United States government has a research agency known as DARPA. The agency is normally funded by the government so that it may develop army helmets that can be used to inflict mind control using ultrasound frequencies.

Mind control is possible depending on the areas of the brain that are being stimulated. It is hoped that the click of a button can manipulate the mind of a soldier as a way of enhancing their fighting capabilities as they go to war. The ultrasonic devices are supposed to be embedded in the helmets that are to be worn by the soldiers, and they can, in turn, transform the soldiers into an unstoppable fighting machine. In theory, the brains of soldiers can be stimulated, and they will not feel any pain, fatigue, or fear. Researchers have been looking into the matter, and they are currently conducting some experiments using worms. At the moment, it is possible to control the direction that the worms travel by using the ultrasound technology that might eventually be used to control soldiers on the battlefield.

Many myths have come up over the years about brainwashing and mind control. As a student, you may be used to analyzing various problems from a certain angle, and you can make your own conclusions in the process.

Daily Mind Control

As a marketer, your focus may be on how you can manipulate different people using different techniques, so that they may bend to your will. Some of the daily mind control techniques that people are subjected to include:

The color of a pill may trick you into thinking that it works effectively.

The scenario in the film *The Matrix* (1999), saw the character Neo being asked to choose between the "red" and "blue" pill. The blue pill would put him to sleep, yet the red pill would ensure that he woke up to "reality." This could be a comment on the apparent psychological impact of color, as many sleeping pills at the pharmacy are indeed blue.

Some people may assume that it is the placebo effect. In this case, the way you perceive different things matters a lot, especially regarding the products that we consume.

MK-ULTRA

The Korean War took place in the 1950s. The war wasn't easy for the United States, and the nation was experiencing some serious challenges, especially when dealing with the Soviet Union. The United States had to look for a way to win the war, and that is when it focused on the human brain. In 1952, the CIA was being led by Allen Dulles. As the director of the CIA, he went ahead to express his concerns about the war.

About MK-Ultra

As the CIA Director, Dulles went ahead to come up with the MK-Ultra Program. The program was classified, and it entailed the use of chemical and biological weapons, sensory deprivation, hypnosis, verbal and sexual abuse, and isolation. Whenever the United States captured a prisoner of war, they would torture them to gain information about the enemy. The prisoners of war would then be rendered incapacitated.

The MK-Ultra program aimed at coming up with a "truth serum" to force information from people who were suspected of being Soviet spies. The CIA was hopeful that it would increase a person's ability to recall some complex pieces of information and the arrangement of various physical objects. The main goals of the MK-Ultra program were to:

1. Produce shock and confusion over extended periods.

2. Cause a victim to age faster or slower.

3. Make it impossible for someone to perform physical activity.

4. Enhance the ability to withstand privation, torture, and coercion during interrogation.

5. Promote illogical thinking and impulsiveness so that a recipient would be discredited in public.

6. Lower ambition and working efficiency.

7. Weaken or distort eyesight or hearing.

8. Increase mental activity and perception.

9. Knock someone out with the use of surreptitiously administered drugs in drinks, food, cigarettes, or as an aerosol.

10. Alter personality structure causing the recipient to become dependent upon another person.

11. Cause temporary or permanent brain damage and loss of memory.

12. Produce physical disablement, such as paralysis of the legs.

13. Produce amnesia for events both preceding and during the experiments and the use of a prisoner.

About LSD

The CIA was conducting MK-Ultra research in colleges, universities, and pharmaceutical companies in North America. The CIA has expressed a specific interest in LSD (lysergic acid diethylamide). The medicine was first discovered in Switzerland, and the drug induces a mental state that is similar to depersonalization, schizophrenia, disintegration, and psychic disorganization. The main effect of the drug was that it could breakdown a person's character defenses for handling instances of anxiety.

The CIA would then administer the drug to its own employees, doctors, military personnel, and government agents without prior knowledge. By doing so, the CIA had violated the Nuremberg Code. The code was introduced after World War II, and it was meant to ensure that human trials would cease. At some point, prisoners were also part of the human trials. People who took LSD would experience a loss of appetite, paranoia, and they would also hallucinate.

Chapter 6: Deception Detection: How to Identify a Lie

Detecting Deception

There are different ways through which you can detect deception in an oral or written statement.

How to Detect an Anomaly

Some professionals have an in-depth understanding of linguistic text analysis. The analysis will entail studying the grammar, language, and syntax, and the main agenda is to learn more about how an event is described, in a bid to detect any anomalies. As an experienced investigator, you will be tasked with detecting some of the nonverbal cues of the subjects. You will focus on eye movement and verbal behavior. Oral statements will also be studied.

Signs of Deception

Some of the signs of deception are as follows:

1. The Lack of Self-Reference

If a person is truthful, they will utilize the pronoun "I" when they are describing what took place. For example, an honest person will go ahead and say, "I arrived home and went straight to the bedroom. After that, I went to talk to my mother, and we had a lengthy chat." That's just an example statement. As we can see, the pronoun "I" appears twice in the statement provided.

Deceptive people will use language that minimizes the number of "I" references. During an oral statement, the witness or suspect may end up leaving out some important pieces of information; this can happen even when they are issuing an informal written statement.

2. Answering a Question with a Question

Even though a person may be a liar, they will prefer not to engage in the act of lying. When a person lies, they risk being detected. Before you answer a question with a lie, you should avoid answering the question at all costs. When trying to act dodgy, people may often answer a question with another question. The investigators should always be on the lookout for people that answer a question with another question.

After talking about deception, we will now look into how to spot a liar. Since the FBI is a security organization, it is well suited to weighing into the matter on how to spot a liar. The following tips may come in handy when spotting a liar:

3. Focus on Building Rapport

It is evident that a "good cop" will always display better results as compared to a "bad cop." During an interview, a person may appear as empathetic, and they will end up gaining access to more information as compared to the person who appears cold. It is also advisable to avoid being accusatory during the interrogation process.

4. Surprising the Suspects

A deceptive individual will always try to anticipate your next move. For instance, they may try to anticipate your next question so that they can ensure each answer they are issuing seems natural. You should always ask those questions that they do not expect.

5. Listening More Than You Speak

If you are a liar, you will focus on speaking more, and your main goal is to ensure that you will sound legitimate. Also, you will focus on winning over a certain target audience. Some liars may make use of some complex sentences so that they can conceal the truth.

You should be aware of the following:

- When people are stressed, they tend to speak faster.
- A stressed person will speak louder.
- The liars usually clear their voice and cough regularly, and that means that they are experiencing some tension.

Although the statements that have been mentioned above are supposed to enlighten you on how to spot a liar, it is good to note that some people may exhibit some signs of tension, but that is not an indicator that they are lying to you. In case you have noticed any of the mentioned actions, you should proceed with caution.

6. Pay Attention to How a Person says, "No"

When engaging a suspect, you should pay close attention to how they utter the word "No." A person depicting some unusual behavior will always face another direction as they say, "No." They may also appear hesitant, and they can also close their eyes.

7. Watch for the Changes in Behavior

When a person changes their behavior, it is an indicator that they may be engaging in deceptive behavior. You should be careful when a person issues some short answers to different questions. Also, they may pretend that they are suffering from memory lapse, especially at a critical moment. They can also start to speak formally, and they may start issuing some exaggerated responses.

8. Always Ask for the Story Backward

If a person is indeed truthful, they will add some details, and they will focus on remembering more stories about what happened. A liar will start by memorizing the story, and they will stick to one narrative. If they add some details, by taking a close look at the details, you will notice that they are not adding up. If you suspect someone is deceptive, you should ask them to recall the event in a backward manner, rather than issuing the narrative from the beginning to the end. You can ask them to talk more about what happened right before a certain point. A person who is telling the truth will usually recall many details. A liar will simplify the story, and they will also contradict themselves.

9. Beware of the Compliments Issued by People

Although compliments are good, they are only good if a genuine person has issued them. You should always be on the lookout for a person who is trying to make a good impression. When you agree with all the opinions being issued by a person and also laugh at all their jokes, it is an indicator that you may be insincere.

10. Asking a Follow-Up Question

People do not like dealing with liars; however, it is good to remember that sometimes people are uneasy with some questions, since they are avoiding instances of personal embarrassment. Also, some people may be extremely dependent on the outcome of a specific conversation.

For instance, during a job interview, a person may be tempted to hide the details about why they may have been fired from their previous job. Although the person may be qualified and their personality is good, they may hide some of these details since they are in dire need of a job. During the interview, a person may issue a response that may seem puzzling. If you are puzzled during an interview by some of the responses, you can come up with some follow-up questions. If you are in doubt, you can continue to ask questions. With time, you will be able to spot whether a person is deceptive or not.

Chapter 7: What Makes a Cult?
10 Brainwashing Tell-Tale Signs

Mind control is a large discipline that covers the subject of cults as well as sects. These are small groups that use deception to control minds while applying tactics to take advantage of the vulnerability of others. These groups also apply several modern and proven tactics that may end up exposing others to danger. These methods are also applied by cult leaders to seek the attention of followers. A one-on-one cult is often defined as an intimate relationship in which an individual abuses their power to manipulate another. It could be a teacher, preacher, or government official. It could also be a therapist who seeks to extort a client. In a different case, it could also be about an abusive and controlling relationship between a couple.

Disintegrating the Cult Psychology

Cults are known for capturing people's attention based on the services and products they claim to offer in the long run. Both fascinating and terrifying, students may want to comprehend the lessons that might be garnered from these "secret" societies. The main question is usually, where does the management come from? What are some of the psychological elements of the cult? Who would live for that? To successfully answer these questions, some people have also been drawn into joining a cult.

With that said, we live in a world filled with challenges where people have abstract issues that need to be solved urgently. As such, these individuals may be vulnerable and end up trying to find various solutions. The same people may look for solutions in the wrong places. According to Dr. Adrian Furnham, who describes the issue in *Psychology Today*, humans are known to crave clarity in all forms possible. Therefore, some people are blinded by the offer of "clarity" from those who would like to take advantage of them. Cults attract people from all backgrounds and ethnicities, but often these people have one thing in common: low self-esteem. They are focused on improving their lives and are manipulated by the often simple messages of cult leaders, who promise the concrete "answers" they seek. The average person is intrigued by the whole idea of a cult and its impact on people's lives.

Many people have also successfully recruited others into their cults to maintain the life of the family tree. Generally, individuals in a cult don't look to recruit people with health issues, such as handicaps or those who are depressed. People with low self-esteem are preferred since they are vulnerable and looking for external approval and answers to make them feel good. Where possible, cults tend to take advantage of other people who are in dire need of community support when it comes to matters of physical and mental well-being. Most of the time, such individuals are compromised in one way or another. Eventually, the idea is to grow a cult's following, to extend its life and relevance. Cults generally aren't motivated to recruit the best of the world's brains, since it may be challenging to control such people.

Once people have been admitted into a cult, they are usually bombarded with love and care. This is a strategy that's commonly used on someone with low self-esteem, as they are flattered, seduced, and complimented; this trains their brain to see the cult as a source of love and acceptance. In the world today, there are many abstract issues that cause people confusion, leading some individuals to seek "concrete" answers within a cult environment. These problems need to be addressed by professional psychologists, who understand how cults are run. Cult leaders are known to promote messages that make sense at that moment in time. Beyond the scenario and in reality, such messages do not make sense. They do not contain any great content that can be substantiated.

Some research suggests that women are more likely to join a cult than men. Why, you may ask?

According to Dr. David Bromley of the prestigious Virginia Commonwealth University, women are intrigued by the fact that they can easily change their lifestyles just by joining a cult. Therefore, this makes them more statistically likely to become members of cults that will victimize them in the long run. This is also because women are more vulnerable and seduced by the appeal of gaining various advantages that have been promised, including access to education as well as funds to take care of their children. It could also be linked to the historical oppression of women. Young women who don't feel independent may sometimes be drawn to a cult; by joining they feel they are "taking charge" of their own life. To such women, it's all about seizing the opportunity and creating a better life for themselves. According to the opinion of many prominent psychologists, such as Dr. Stanley H. Cath, many of these cult members need treatment after being immersed in a cult. From his first-hand experience, it's clear that this is an interesting trend affecting masses of people in different parts of the world. Many individuals joining cults have experienced religion in their lives. They have also rejected it. Maybe this is pretty surprising to some extent, since cults are known for being religious. In the opinion of Dr. Cath, it's clear that this is a trend and a major sign of a deeper issue that needs to be addressed in society. Some of the individuals who end up joining cults are intelligent and successful in business, for example. Other than that, many people who have joined these cults are known for being exposed to emotional and physical abuse at some point in their lives.

Cults and secret societies are powerful, since they isolate members from their initial lives that were not cult-related. They break down a person's former identity and build a new one, cultivating a mentality of "us" versus "them." As such, leaders of a cult will tend to convince their victims to separate themselves from the society in which they grew up. To successfully achieve this, the cult leader is generally charming, and has to master the tactics of mind control and how to apply them for their personal gain.

Ten signs that you are in a cult include:

1. The Leader is Normally the Ultimate Authority

If you are not in a position to criticize your leader, it means that you are possibly in a cult. Charismatic leaders are the ones that form cults, and they always claim that they possess some special knowledge. In some instances, they may refer to themselves as "messiahs" or "messengers." Charismatic cult leaders may also manifest in the form of military officials, executives within a company, or even politicians. Cult leaders normally convince their members to ignore critical thinking, so they have a sense of belonging, purpose, and authority over them. Members are not allowed to question the evidence that is presented by the cult leader. The leader is always right, and they should never be questioned even when they mislead the flock. It is forbidden to criticize the leaders.

2. The Group Suppresses Skepticism

If you can only study your organization using approved sources, there is a possibility that you are in a cult. Cults usually view critical thinking as a threat, and they focus on suppressing it. If you are one of the doubting members, you will be encouraged to isolate yourself from the others so that you cannot subject them to some undue influence. You should focus mainly on the doctrines of the cult. In a cult, you are prohibited from criticizing the leaders. The members of a cult are also forbidden from consuming material that does not align with the cult's doctrines.

3. The Group Can Delegitimize Former Members

If you are finding it difficult to leave a certain group, it is an indicator that you may be part of a cult. The cult normally considers itself as the chief authority, and it does not want members to leave at any given moment. Cult leaders usually come up with false narratives that are meant to deceive members and deter them from leaving. If a member speaks out, they are perceived as bitter, evil, dishonest, and angry. Cults will shun members who go against the doctrines, to prevent them from influencing other members.

4. The Group May Be Paranoid about the Outside World

If a group starts to talk about the end of the world being near, it is an indicator that they may be part of a cult. The cult will position itself to make members believe that the evil from the outside world cannot affect them. Such cults usually thrive on conspiracy theories, persecution complexes, and catastrophic thinking. In a bid to attract more members, these cults ensure that they are aggressive while recruiting people. They can also claim that they are "saving" people from the evil that is present in the world. When a person rejects the message of the cult, they are termed as "stupid" or "evil."

5. The Group Depends Greatly on Shame Cycles

If you normally rely on your group so that you may feel loved, sufficient, or worthy, it means that you are in a cult. Cult leaders normally focus on ensuring that they have trapped their members in shame cycles. They will impose a code of conduct that is strict. They will come up with prescriptions about appearance, diet, and relationships. By members of the cult guilt-tripping other members, they position themselves as unique. When one of the members feels unworthy, they will start to talk more about their shortcomings to the cult leader. The leader will use this opportunity to further entrench their power over the member, and they will decide whether the member is worthy or not.

6. Cult Leaders Are Usually Above the Law

Cult leaders tend to assume that they are above the law, and that is why they focus more on exploiting their members sexually and economically, and there are no repercussions. When a cult leader is apprehended and confronted, they will fail to confess their wrongdoings. They will come up with justifications as to why they engage in different acts. A loyal cult member will also try to justify the behavior of their leader.

7. The Group May Use Certain Methods to Reform the Thoughts of Members

The leaders of a cult will always make use of different brainwashing techniques so that they can break down the sense of identity of each member and their ability to think straight. The members will engage in behaviors such as prayer, fasting, scripture reading, meditation, chanting, and also at times drug abuse. At the end of it all, the person will be vulnerable, and they will more easily respond to the suggestions posed by the cult leaders. These thought-terminating methods have proven to be effective, and people will then follow their leaders blindly. The cult members will also fail to analyze some of the complex issues that may come about from time to time.

8. The Group is Elitist

If the group you are in is the "solution" to different problems in the world, it means that you are part of a cult. Cults usually view themselves as enlightened, and they transform different individuals radically throughout the globe. Elitism usually creates some form of responsibility and unity, and it is centered on a united purpose. Cult leaders can also manipulate followers to take part in subservient behaviours, such as sexual favors, risky financial behavior, and free manual labor.

9. Financial Transparency Does Not Exist

If you are not allowed to know more about what happens with the money in a group, it means you are in a cult. The group may fail to disclose how the finances are being used, and that raises a red flag. Cult leaders will continue to lead their dream life, and the followers will be tasked with making financial contributions from time to time. The members will also be encouraged to contribute some money regardless of their situation.

10. The Group May Be Performing Secret Rites

In a cult, some secret teachings may exist. If you are not in a cult, you may assume that the existence of secret rites are more of a myth; however, after joining a cult, you will learn about the reality of the ceremonies and secret teachings involved. Cults utilize the secret ceremonies as a rite of passage, and it is meant to solidify the loyalty of members. The initiation takes place after a member has taken part in different tests. In some instances, the member is only required to make a financial contribution. Cult initiations are somewhat bizarre and confusing. After the rite of passage, members of the cult become more loyal, since they are now a part of the "inner circle." These members are more susceptible, especially after undergoing the rite of passage to cement their membership in a cult.

Chapter 8: Media Manipulation: Strategies and How to See Through Them

Media Manipulation

Some of the tactics and techniques that are used by various media outlets include psychological manipulation, logical fallacies, the use of rhetorical questions, the use of propaganda, and outright deception. The main focus of this kind of media organization is on suppressing the information and the points of view of the target population, while dictating what their options and thoughts should be. Some people will be forced to listen to specific one-sided arguments. People's attention may also be diverted elsewhere, away from the real issues.

Some of the media manipulation strategies that are currently in use will be discussed in this section. There is indeed a huge number of people who may not be aware of "media manipulation." Although people lack basic knowledge about what media manipulation entails, some researchers have taken the bold step to come up with a list of different techniques that are used by deceptive individuals, such as politicians and media outlets that support them, since they want to control the public.

When looking into different media manipulation techniques, the main focus is on learning more about the techniques used when carrying out mass manipulation. Media manipulation strategies work to ensure that people are submissive, docile, obedient, and don't think for themselves. Additionally, some media outlets can support inequality, capitalism, and neo-capitalism.

Some of the popular media manipulation techniques are as follows:

1. Distraction

The distraction strategy is meant to deviate the target population from focusing on the important issues that pose significance in their lives. To ensure that people are distracted, media houses can flood the news with stories that revolve around trivial issues. The main objective is to ensure that the people are distracted by making sure that their minds are occupied. The end result is that people will stop asking questions about why the media is not looking into specific issues. In the process, people will even forget the real issues.

2. Problem-Reaction-Solution

This method can be likened to how politicians try to lure voters during an election period. The population is normally tested first. The first step is to spread rumors, and an evaluation will be carried out to assess how the general population reacts. After creating a problem, the second phase involves offering a solution to the problem. The public will view the manipulators as heroes.

3. Gradualism

This is the process of manipulating people by ensuring that they have accepted some socially unjust decisions. The population is manipulated gradually. The gradual manipulation may take place for many years.

4. Differing

Another strategy used by the media is differing; this is the instance whereby people present some unpopular decisions, and they may emphasize that the decisions should be implemented since the general population will benefit significantly. The public may believe everything genuinely, and they may make some sacrifices, which they believe will bring forth some significant changes. For instance, the politicians may be the manipulators in this case, and they may trick the voters into thinking that they will lead a better life after the polls. At the end of it all, the people will realize that no changes have been implemented and they lose faith and disengage with the system.

5. Treating People like Children

The media may be focusing on manipulating the public regularly. When they manipulate the public continuously, it is an indicator that they are treating people like children. The media will try to brainwash people through the use of sugarcoated arguments, intonations, and characters. The media will, in turn, assume that people are immature, and they are incapable of handling the truth. The main goal is to ensure that the target audience is docile, submissive, and they are reacting as planned. Media manipulation ensures that people cannot think like adults.

6. Appealing to People's Emotions

The media has learned more about how to appeal to people's emotions, and their main focus is on ensuring that people are unable to think critically. Various media outlets that want to push an agenda want to control people's thoughts. You should look into how powerful fear is as a tool.

7. Keeping the Public Mediocre and Ignorant

Some media organizations prefer dealing with people who are uncultured and also ignorant. By ensuring that people are isolated from various pieces of knowledge, the media can easily manipulate the public, this is also true for certain politicians. The media also ensures that a rebellion does not take place since people are ignorant.

8. Encouraging the Public to Accept Mediocrity

By ensuring that the public accepts mediocrity, it is similar to ensuring that the general population is ignorant. The media prefers to make use of such strategies when manipulating people. For instance, is the media airing the shows that people want to watch? Are some shows imposed on us by the media? In short, do we get to consume the content that we want, or does the media impose different pieces of content on us? At times it is clear that the media is brainwashing us, and we have ceased to care much about our surroundings. Also, we have been trained to be mediocre.

9. Self-Blame

The media usually encourages self-blame and ignorance and also makes sure that people believe that they are responsible for their own misfortunes. In short, the media will focus on self-incrimination, and will make sure that the public will not mobilize at all costs.

10. Completing the Knowledge of the Public

To control the general public, the media has focused on learning more about its audience. The media can work together with other companies to learn more about every individual in an attempt to easily manipulate the masses.

It is advisable to learn more about how to spot media manipulation. The resources talking about how to spot media manipulation are few; as a result, we cannot delve into the topic in an in-depth manner. However, pay attention and you may notice now when various media outlets are trying to manipulate people.

Chapter 9: Political Propaganda: Tools, Mechanisms, and Ways to Avoid It

Political Propaganda – this is defined as people spreading false information because they support a particular cause. Propaganda is presented negatively, especially when dealing with politicians, since they often make false claims so that they can lure citizens into voting for them.

Techniques and How Political Propaganda Works

During the election period, politicians are supposed to campaign. They will talk about what they will do for the citizens. In turn, people will vote for them. After assuming office, the politicians may fail to heed their promises. People who are disappointed may vow never to vote for them again. Surprisingly, the politicians will make use of political propaganda, and commonly the people will end up voting for the same politicians.

Present political propaganda techniques have proven to be greatly effective. Nowadays, people making use of political propaganda are focusing on symbolism. When targeting the mind of a voter, you should also hit their heart. Politicians will also make use of generalizations, and they will make sure that some things sound great. On the surface, things may look good, but when you dig deeper, you will realize that the people making use of propaganda are trying to deceive all their followers.

The Tools of Propaganda

A propagandist will always make use of certain tools so that they can mobilize some followers. The most important tool is suggestion, and it aligns with stimulation. The propagandists will stimulate other people to accept all they have to say without challenging their assertions. Since stimulation is a propaganda device, it makes sure that people can accept all the propositions that are brought forth without even thinking logically.

The propagandist will make use of this tool by coming up with some positive statements that are meant to entice a group of people. They will always present their statements using a familiar language, and they will ensure that they have incorporated simplicity in each instance. By failing to admit the reality, the propagandist will be able to amass a huge following.

Suggestion is also used in the advertising sector. Another commonly used tool is insinuations, hints, and indirect statements. The best example, in this case, is the advertisement sector. One example is political advertisements, which are often pure propaganda with manipulated "facts" or outright deceptions.

Another tool is when a propagandist focuses on learning more about people, in order to know how to appeal to and manipulate his target audience.

Looking into Social Media Tools

Social media ensures that people can keep in contact through the use of applications such as Facebook. For instance, there is a group of young individuals that learned about the Tinder dating app, and they began to influence their colleagues. With time, some of the conversations within the platform would be more about politics.

On various social media sites, certain propagandists send messages targeting various voters with mis-information. The users of these sites had agreed to the terms and conditions while signing up. It is not clear how many candidates manage to win elections by carrying out social media campaigns.

Nowadays, social media is among the online applications that are widely used. About 70 percent of adults in the United States have signed up on Facebook. A huge percentage of the people who have signed up on Facebook and different social media applications log into these platforms regularly. The majority of the people are also not using social media platforms for politics; they are using these platforms rather for self-expression, finding articles, and sharing content.

Social media has become common, and it is a major part of people's lives. It is also trusted, unregulated, and targetable. Since social media has attracted a considerable population, politicians were bound to make use of such tools during the election period. There is a substantial amount of evidence that social media is being used to deceive and manipulate voters.

Since technology has also advanced greatly, the news feed is also automated, and that means that the politicians may focus on manipulating different social networks. The best example, in this case, is the manner in which about half of the Twitter conversations globally usually originate from bots. Some of these accounts contain a substantial amount of political content. The political content has been well crafted, such that the targets will not realize that they are chatting with a bot.

Some of these bots have been used in other nations such as Brazil during the election period. The bots were used during the period when one of the presidents was being impeached. They came in handy when carrying out the impeachment campaign. Also, the bots were used during the mayoral race that took place in Rio. The majority of political leaders are also making use of social media tools, especially in young democracies that are utilizing automation in a bid to spread information.

Chapter 10: Psychological Warfare: Don't Be Manipulated

When it comes to manipulation, the manipulator will always focus on getting what they want, using various forms of trickery. Many people believe that manipulation is immoral. Since psychological manipulators use various deception techniques, we will look into each of these tactics and offer a suitable solution on how people can defend themselves in case of any eventuality.

Method 1 – Gaining Manipulation Skills

1. Take an Acting Class

When it comes to manipulation, it is good to learn more about how to master emotions while making sure that other people can become receptive, whenever you tend to become emotional. To learn more about expressing yourself using various techniques that play on people's emotions, it is good to enroll in an acting class. While in an acting class, it will be possible to gain some powers of persuasion. Always focus on the main goal, which involves understanding the methods of manipulating people, so you can protect yourself.

2. Enroll in a Public Speaking Class

The acting classes are meant to make sure that you can master your emotions and how you display them. The main reason why enrolling for a debate class is advisable is because you will be able to learn more about convincing other people about your argument. You will learn more about how to organize your thoughts clearly. Additionally, a public speaking class will also enlighten you about how to sound convincing. A manipulative person will use these skills to influence the actions of others by convincing them to do what they want.

3. Come up with Similarities

Manipulators always make sure that they have learned more about the body language of their target victims. They also look into the intonation patterns of their victims before they can proceed with the manipulation process. Eventually, the manipulators will come up with persuasive methods, and they will also appear calm. Watch out for this type of behavior.

4. Being Charismatic

Charismatic individuals often have a way of getting what they want. When understanding how charming people can manipulate others, you will have to ensure that you have worked on your own charisma. Not everyone who is charismatic is manipulative, so pay attention to understand who is sincere and who is misleading you. You should also be able to smile, and your body language should showcase that you are approachable, so that people feel they can easily approach you and talk to you. You must also be able to initiate a conversation with any individual, regardless of various factors, such as age. Some of the techniques that you can utilize to become charismatic include:

- Ensuring that people feel special. The best way to achieve this is through maintaining eye contact while conversing with a person. Make sure that you have also initiated a discussion about how they feel and the interests that they have. Always show the other person that you care, and you want to learn more about them. An insincere charismatic person will pretend to care about the other person, even when they don't.

• Always maintain high levels of confidence. Charismatic people are always passionate about everything that they do. It is also advisable to have confidence in yourself.

5. Learn from the Masters

If you have a friend who happens to be a psychological manipulator, you should observe them and also take notes, so you know what to look out for from potential manipulators. Always carry out a case study and ensure that the manipulators are the main point of focus. It will be possible to learn a lot from them. Pay attention to how these individuals get what they want. They may also share some insight into how they manipulate people. The main issue is that you might end up being tricked, but you will gain some insight into how to manipulate people effectively, and therefore how to avoid being manipulated.

6. Learn More about How to Read People

Each individual has a psychological and emotional makeup, and it always varies from one individual to another. When you learn about the psychological and emotional makeup of a person, it will be possible to manipulate them. People who are manipulative will often learn more about the individual that they are going to manipulate, and in many cases they become trusted by the person before they slowly take advantage of them. Some of the things that you may notice as you try to understand people include:

• Most people are vulnerable, and it is possible to reach out to them by evoking their emotional responses. For instance, some people may cry when watching a movie, and they may showcase high levels of sympathy and empathy. For a person to manipulate such individuals, they often joke around with their emotions while also pretending to feel sorry, and they will eventually get what they want by playing on the other person's emotions.

• Other people have a strong sense of guilt. Most of the individuals who have a guilt reflex grew up in a restrictive household, and they may have been punished for every wrong deed that they committed. Manipulators may make sure that the person feels guilty about various acts, so they are more likely to give in to a manipulator's demands at the end of it all.

• Some people usually respond to rational approaches. For example, if you have a close friend who is always logical and always keeps up with the news, that means that they are always after verifiable information. In such an instance, a manipulative person will make sure that they have utilized their persuasive powers accordingly when manipulating them.

Method 2 – Using Different Manipulation Techniques

1. Impose an Unreasonable Request, Then Present a Reasonable One

This is a technique that has proven to be very effective, and many manipulators often use it. It is also shockingly simple. Whenever a person wants to manipulate someone, they come up with a request that is not reasonable. The other person will reject the unreasonable request, and in that instance, a reasonable request is presented. The new request should be appealing to the individual who is being targeted. The best example to use in such a case is when an employee may not accept a permanent request to arrive early at work, but they will voluntarily accept a request whereby they are supposed to arrive at work early over a specific period of time to handle various urgent duties. The employee will prefer engaging in a short-term request, since it is less cumbersome when compared to the long-term request.

2. Inspire Fear, Then Ensure That the Victim Has a Sense of Relief

A manipulator may have chosen their victims carefully, based on who is the most vulnerable. In this case, a manipulative person will make sure that a victim's worst fears have come to life. In the process, they will then focus on ensuring that these fears are relieved, and the victim will be happy enough to give them what they want. This kind of manipulation is dangerous and you should reach out to people who can help to keep you safe from an abusive dynamic like this.

An example of how this kind of behavior might begin – assume that you have a car. Your friend might try to shock you by telling you that the car was producing some funny noises and that the engine might be dead. At that juncture, you will be in fear. After that, they inform you that they realized the strange noise was being produced by the radio. You are relieved. Since you are relieved, your friend may go ahead and ask for another favor, such as – they want to borrow the car again.

3. Ensure That a Person Feels Guilty

A manipulator may try to get what they want by invoking guilt in another person. For starters, they might carry out an evaluation and learn more about how to make someone feel guilty, by making that person feel bad for a variety of reasons.

If the manipulator is targeting their parents, for example, they would showcase that it's their parents' fault that they are the way they are in that moment.

If invoking some form of guilt among one of their friends, they may make sure that they have enlightened their friend about the number of times that they have been let down by them.

4. Bribe a Person

When a manipulative person is after something, they may issue a bribe. In such an instance, they do not have to use tactics such as blackmail to get what they want. A reward may be given but in the form of a bribe. The manipulator will learn more about your needs but will try to hide the fact that they are issuing a bribe.

5. Pretend That You Are the Victim

When a manipulative person pretends that they are a victim, they will attract some sympathy. This is a commonly used method for some people, who "play" the victim any chance they get. They usually make sure that they don't overdo the act in an attempt to get what they are looking for at the end of it all. Victims always appear helpless, and that means that the target will appear vulnerable as they offer to help them. They will pretend to be dumb, although they know what they are doing. They may pretend to be pathetic and helpless but will get more desperate and even enraged if you realize and don't give in to this type of emotional manipulation. You need to try to discern who is a real victim and who is manipulating you.

6. Use Logic

Logic is important in some of the day to day activities that you engage in. Always ensure that you have come up with a list of reasons as to why you would benefit from the things that you are asking for from someone. A manipulative person will always present their case, calmly and rationally, but they will make sure to display some emotions, to get what they want at the end of it all.

7. Maintain the Character

Depending on the method that has been used, a manipulator will try to make sure that they have displayed some emotions that could relate to their current scenario.

They may appear worried or even upset, depending on the matter at hand.

Method 3 – Manipulate Anyone in Your Life

As a manipulator, a person may develop different tendencies, including manipulating other people who are close to them in real life.

1. Manipulating Your Friends

When it comes to manipulating or being manipulated by your friends, you might realize that it is a tricky situation. Perhaps your friend has been making sure to flatter you, always making sure that they have been nice while also doing some small favors, in case they need a favor within a few days. If someone is a "real" friend they won't need to manipulate you for a favor, and vice versa. Try to stay away from toxic "friends." Some ways that the manipulation may be carried out:

- Utilize your emotions - your friends should be caring individuals; as a result, they will not want to see you upset. If you have any acting skills, make sure that you have used them accordingly to ensure that you will appear to be a very upset individual.

- Constantly remind your friend about how good they are - always ensure that you remember the periods when you have always done some good things for the sake of your friend.

- Guilt-trip your friends - you do not have to utilize the "bad friend" card. Always mention someone casually and remind them about how they have let you down. Always make it sound like your friend is uncaring without going overboard.

2. Manipulating Your Significant Other

If you have a manipulative partner, they may attempt to gain favors by turning you on and asking for the favor, so you understand you cannot get what you want unless you heed their demands. They may try "buttering you up" by asking for favors after giving you compliments or lightening the mood. These examples are the kind of thing that might happen, before more damaging behavior escalates. You should try not to get too deeply involved with a romantic partner who is manipulative as it is possible they will be abusive in other ways.

3. The Impression You Use Determines Whether Your Manipulation Techniques Will Subdue the Target

A manipulative person will always make sure that they are deceptive and also swift. What matters most to them is ensuring that their image is still intact.

• Utilize emotions – look into what your significant other would do when they realize that you are wallowing in sorrow. In most cases, your partner will ensure that they have reignited the happiness within you.

• Public embarrassment – if your partner is determined to solicit a favor from you, they may have utilized the waterworks approach in a public place. The best example to showcase the effectiveness of such an approach is – when a child tries to solicit a favor from their parents in public, the child hopes the parent will give in to their demands. This technique will most likely be used sparingly.

• Issue small bribes – to encourage a favor, such as going out on a dinner date or to any other event, small bribes might be used.

4. Manipulating Your Boss

When dealing with professional relationships, for example in an employee / manager dynamic, there are some things that can be done to increase the chance of a positive working relationship and of you being able to appropriately appeal to your boss for what you want from time to time. Use the approaches that are logical and rational when dealing with your boss. When you have some personal problems, do not discuss them in front of your boss. Also, do not appear at your boss's desk crying because of some personal issues.

There is a high chance that you will be fired. When dealing with your boss, make sure that you are logical. Also, make sure that you have provided some good reasons regarding why you need some assistance from your boss.

- Make sure that you are a model worker. Such a technique will always work when you need to make a request. Also, make sure that you are working a bit late. Additionally, make sure that you are always happy and smiling whenever you are around your boss.

- When soliciting a favor from your boss, make sure that you have done so in an offhand manner. Always request casually. For instance, approach your boss in the office and tell them that there is an important matter that you wanted to discuss with them. When your boss hears that, they will issue you their undivided attention, and they will enact on your favor at the end of the day.

- Try to ask for a favor at the end of the day. Do not engage your boss early in the morning. First, make sure that you have observed their mood. If they showcase that they are stressed, you could opt for another moment. If you want to approach your boss during a break, you can do so as they go to look for lunch. They will want to quickly deal with your requests, and they will not also argue with you.

5. Manipulating the Teacher

If you want to manipulate your teacher, you must do so professionally. Also, make sure that you have incorporated some emotions. During the specific day that you want to make a request, you should make sure that you have appeared before the teacher as a model student. Also, make sure that you have arrived in class early. Try to ensure that the teacher can notice that you have been reading a lot. In short, the teacher should note that you are taking your studies seriously. While in the classroom, make sure that you are active, and you should be focused.

- Always enlighten the teacher about how great they are, and you should do so casually. Tell them about how they inspire you. In some instances, also ensure that you have enlightened them about how much you love the subjects that they are teaching.

- Mention some stuff about what is happening at home. Although the situation might appear to be awkward, the teacher will be able to sympathize with you since they will feel sorry, and they might want to learn more about your situation.

- As you discuss your personal life, ensure that you have done so in a strategic manner, and your teacher will eventually become uncomfortable. If you had delayed when it comes to issuing your assignment, the teacher might have some pity on you because of your situation, and they will offer you an extension, which means you can submit your assignment later. If the teacher refuses to grant you an extension, always enlighten them that you understand that they do not extend the period when the students should hand in their assignments. Your voice should appear to be frail since you want the teacher to sympathize with you. There is a high chance that the teacher will give in to your demands.

- If such a technique does not work, you can choose to cry, since you must demonstrate that you are indeed emotional. You will start crying, and the teacher will become uncomfortable, and that means that they will be more likely to heed to your commands.

6. Manipulating Your Parents

It is evident that your parents should always love you, unconditionally. As a result, they may be more susceptible to manipulation techniques. The main fact here is that your parents love you, and they will always support you in every way possible. You have to ensure that you are a model offspring for some time before you can make a request involving certain favors. Always make sure that you have not missed your curfew. Also, make sure that you have spent most of your time studying and assisting in handling some house chores. Afterward, you can go ahead and request a favor.

- Ensure that your request is reasonable. For instance, you may want to attend a concert and the following day you should be attending school. When making such a request, make sure that you have done so casually. Always make sure that your parents can see the possibility in the situation, and they will not reject the proposal in the long run.

- You can also pose a question to your parents while you are folding laundry. When handling such tasks, your parents will remember that they have a great son or a daughter, and they will be more likely to comply with your wishes.

- Talk more about how you will engage in some of these activities together with your friends. When your parents hear that you will be engaging in a specific activity together with your friends, they will be more inclined to issue you the go-ahead to proceed.

- Ensure that your parents feel guilty. For instance, you may have wanted to go to a concert. If your parents deny you the opportunity to take part in such an event, you will just tell them that it's okay. Always make sure that your parents will feel guilty since you may be missing out on an opportunity to take part in a major event.

How to Defend Yourself from Manipulative Individuals

For starters, it is good to note that it is not possible to defend yourself from a manipulative individual. The best thing that you can do in this case is to make sure that you have first identified that the individual is indeed manipulative. If they happen to showcase that they are deceptive, you should ensure that you have kept a safe distance from these individuals. If they are not deceptive, you can continue being friends. It is also good to note that some people may mislead others by spreading false information. For example, you may come across some people talking about how manipulative a certain person is, but they are the ones trying to manipulate you and your opinion of this other person.

Never issue the manipulative person a warning. If you notice early on, you should just leave and continue leading your life as usual. After leaving them, they will look for other individuals who they can manipulate into ensuring that they have heeded their demands. If a person is unwell, you should go ahead and try to find out more about their condition. Since some people do lie, you can also go ahead and seek some expert advice from a psychologist or even a psychiatrist. If the person is unwell and they do not showcase any signs of improvement, you can move on and continue living your life as usual, if they are not threatening you.

If the manipulative individual is related to you, you should always be direct with them. Ensure that you have set some boundaries and always be firm so that they cannot dare to cross the set boundaries. Manipulative individuals will realize that they will be held accountable once they tend to showcase undesirable behaviors. How such people behave toward you will also determine how you interact with them.

If they understand some of the rules that you have set, they will in some cases be okay with that, and they will not intrude in any way. Also, ensure that you have initiated a discussion with the manipulative individual while also trying to learn more about their character and condition. Ensure that you have not lectured them in any way. Always ask questions that will help you to learn more about how they are. Never try to fix them, leave such matters to professionals such as psychiatrists or psychologists. Always ensure that you have issued them a referral to a renowned psychiatrist or any other medical practitioner who can deal with their condition accordingly. The manipulative individuals should also be issued the support that they need.

Although some of the stories issued by the manipulative individuals will appear far-fetched, you should never judge them. According to them, their story is valid, although it may appear to be made up to some extent. Ensure that you have not told them any of your stories. If anything goes wrong, they will always use the information that they have about you to fight back. Always remember that we never choose our family members; as a result, you should choose whether you will help them or ignore them. If any other people may appear to be toxic in your life, you should also avoid them. Manipulation and abuse in romantic and other close relationships can build up with "small" occurrences, and they can end with an attempt at total control of one person over another. This is very dangerous and damaging, and you must be on alert in the early stages of manipulative behavior, to be able to get free of this kind of dynamic before it becomes totally destructive. Always seek help if you feel you need it, to stay safe from a threatening and abusive individual, as some situations escalate to an unsafe level.

How to Know If You are Being Manipulated and How to Defend Yourself

Psychological manipulation usually breeds some form of healthy social influence, and it usually occurs between many individuals. The relationships, in this case, are usually give or take. In psychological manipulation, one person will always benefit from the other by taking advantage of them. The individual manipulating the other always does it deliberately, and they often bring about an imbalance of power since they are exploiting other people for their own self-benefit.

The characteristics of manipulative individuals are;

- They know how to detect the weaknesses of other people.
- Once they identify a person's weaknesses, they will always use these weaknesses against them.
- They will always convince the victims to give up something so that they may serve their self-centered interests.

- Once a manipulative individual manages to take advantage of another person, they will always violate the other party until the exploited person ensures that the manipulation spree has come to an end.

Some of the causes of chronic manipulation are always deep-seated and complex. However, it is not easy to identify the main drive that causes a person to be manipulative psychologically. Also, when a person is being manipulated, they do encounter different challenges. The main question that arises, in this case, is how people manage such a situation. Some of the best ways to handle manipulative individuals include:

1. Make Sure You Are Conversant with Your Human Rights

When dealing with a psychologically manipulative individual, make sure that you know more about your human rights. It would be easy to recognize when any of your rights are being violated. Also, make sure that you are not harming other individuals. Every person has a right to stand up for themselves, while also defending each of their rights. If you harm other people, you may be violating each of these human rights. Some of the important rights include:

- The right to be treated with respect.
- The right to express opinions, feelings, and wants.
- The right to set your own priorities.
- The right to say "no" without feeling guilty.
- The right to get anything that you pay for.
- The right to have a different opinion from that of your colleagues.
- The right to protect yourself from being mistreated mentally, physically, or emotionally.
- The right to always create your own happiness while also living a healthy life.

All these human rights are meant to represent a boundary that should never be crossed by the manipulative individuals.

It is evident that our society has many people who do not respect the rights of others. Some of these psychological manipulators always want to exploit people's rights so that they may take advantage of them in every way possible. The main important thing to note is that we all have the right to declare that *we* have the power over ourselves, since most people might assume that the manipulator is the one with the power. The manipulative individual does not have any power over you whatsoever.

2. Keep Your Distance

One of the most effective ways to identify a person who is a manipulator is by observing how various individuals behave when they are around you and when they are around other individuals. If the individual happens to behave differently when they are around different people, this is a character trait that symbolizes they might be manipulative. Everyone has a degree of social differentiation, and some psychological manipulators may prove to be extreme in different instances. Or they may be polite to various individuals while being extremely rude to others. They may also seem helpless, and in other instances, they will showcase some aggressiveness. When you observe such character traits regularly, you should always keep your distance. Avoid engaging such people unless you are forced to depending on the circumstances. It was earlier mentioned that it is difficult to learn more about why people tend to be psychologically manipulative. As a result, ensure that you have kept your distance since such individuals cannot be saved from their current predicaments.

3. Avoid Self-Blame and Personalization

In most cases, manipulative individuals tend to look for a person's weakness, and they will start exploiting them afterward. The people who are being exploited may feel inadequate, and they may also indulge in some self-blame since they may have failed to satisfy the manipulator in different ways. In some of these situations, it is good to note that although you are being manipulated, you are not the problem. The manipulator is taking advantage of you while also ensuring that you feel bad about yourself. You may surrender all your rights and power to the manipulative individuals. Always ask yourself questions such as:

- Are you being treated with the respect that you deserve?
- Are the demands of the manipulative person reasonable?
- Is the relationship beneficial to one party or both parties?
- Do you feel good about the relationship?

4. Focus on Asking Probing Questions

Psychological manipulators will always issue demands to each of the individuals that they are manipulating. Some of the "offers" that they put across will seem unreasonable to some extent, but they will expect you to meet all their needs. Whenever you feel like you are being solicited unreasonably, it is good to focus on yourself by also asking the manipulator different probing questions. To look into whether each of these individuals has some self-awareness, they will recognize the inequity that is present in each of their schemes. Some of the suitable probing questions include:

- Is the relationship reasonable?
- Does what the manipulator want seem fair?
- Do you have a say in the relationship?
- Are you gaining anything?
- What are your expectations?

When you ask yourself some of these questions, you will be coming up with a mirror that is meant to show you the reality. The questions are meant to ensure that the manipulator can see the reality about their nature. In an instance whereby the manipulator has some form of self-awareness, they will withdraw the demands that they have been putting across, and they will back down. Some pathological manipulators can also be termed as narcissists, and they will dismiss each of the questions being directed to them. They will always insist you are getting in their way. If you ever find yourself in such a scenario, always ensure that you have applied different ideas that will ensure you have outsmarted the manipulative individuals. By being creative, you can hopefully bring an end to the manipulation spree.

5. Utilize Time to Your Advantage

Besides making some unreasonable requests, the manipulator will always ask questions and expect an immediate answer in each case. They will always exert some undue pressure while also striving to control the situation. The best example is people who are engaging in sales. Their main aim is to ensure that they have marketed different products successfully, and they may be manipulative so that people may purchase each of the products that they are selling. In such an instance, the manipulative individual will expect you to answer each of their questions immediately. They will also take advantage in different ways while also distancing themselves from the immediate influence that they have brought forth. Always exercise some sense of leadership by telling the manipulative individual that you will think about it and issue them an answer at an opportune moment.

Some of these words always prove to be powerful, and since we have used an example of sales agents, the customer, in this case, is the one who is supposed to address the salesperson and tell them that they will think about it. Always take time to think about the merits and demerits that may be present, depending on the current situation. Also, try to look into whether it is possible to come up with an equitable arrangement, or you should say no, depending on the current scenario.

6. Always Learn to Say "No"

It is not easy to say "no," however, you should first learn the art of communication. When you effectively learn to say "no," you will be able to stand your ground while also making sure that you have been able to maintain a workable relationship. Also, make sure that you are conversant with your human rights, most importantly the area that involves making sure that you can set your own priorities without incurring any form of guilt. After all, you have the right to choose your own happiness and a healthy life too. Always make sure that you can resist while keeping your peace.

7. Always Confront the Bullies

A psychological manipulator tends to become a bully at some point. They will always intimidate or harm their victims. The most important point to note is that the bullies will always prey on the individuals that they may perceive as weak. The manipulative individuals will go ahead with the exploitation whenever they come across an individual who is compliant and passive. When you make yourself a worthy target, the manipulative individuals will not hesitate to pounce on you. It is also evident that a majority of the people who enjoy bullying are also cowards. Whenever a person begins to showcase that they know their rights, the bullies will always back down. Various studies have also been carried out, and it is evident that most of the bullies have also been victims of violence at some point in their lives. Although the bullies have also been victimized at some point in their lives, it is not an excuse as to why they are bullying others. Such information is meant to ensure that you can view bullies from a different perspective.

When you confront a bully, you will be confident enough that you can protect yourself against various forms of danger. You may stand tall as an individual while also supporting other individuals when they are bullied. In an instance whereby a person has been psychologically, emotionally, or verbally assaulted, always make sure that you have sought the services of a counselor and also report the matters to the legal authorities, and they will take the necessary course of action. Always make sure that you can stand up to the bullies, and you may partner with some individuals who are fed up with practices such as bullying.

8. Set Consequences

When an individual who thrives on manipulation insists on violating your personal boundaries, always make sure that you are in a position to tell them "no." Always make sure that you are in a position to assert and also identify consequences. Possession of such knowledge can ensure that you can handle difficult people. When a bully understands the consequences that may come about as a result of their actions, always make sure that they can learn more about the value of respect.

Chapter 11: Workspace Manipulators: Spot Them and Stop Them

Deception Tactics at the Workplace – How to Influence People

Influencing tactics can be grouped into three categories; these are emotional, logical, or cooperative appeals. In simpler terms, it is influencing the head, heart, or hands.

❖ **Logical Appeal** – this is tapping into people's rational and intellectual sides. In this category, you will present your argument for the best course of action basing it on organizational or personal benefits, or both, which is appealing to people's minds.

❖ **Emotional Appeal** – this connects your message, goal, or project to individual goals and values. This can be by outlining ideas that promote one's feelings of well-being, service, or to achieve a sense of belonging, which tugs at the heart; hence, the chances are that it will gain much-needed support from the rest of the team.

❖ **Cooperative Appeals** – this can be translated to mean "collaboration," which is, *what are those tasks that you will do together?* While consultation involves the *ideas* that other people have, it's important to build alliances with those who have already given their support to you or who have much-needed credibility. That is why coming together for a common purpose in an organization can work wonders, because extending a hand to others can be a very effective tool when it comes to influencing.

Note that in any organization or any other place for that matter, leaders who can master these influencing skills and effectively use them can achieve their goals and objectives more successfully and amicably than leaders who lack these skills, irrespective of their management positions in that particular organization.

Which Influence Tactic Is Right for You?

You should consider the following tactics below when choosing the influence that will work best for you:

✔ **Know Your Audience.** Identify and understand each of your stakeholders. This is because each has his/her own agenda and set of special concerns and issues, perspectives, and priorities. Moreover, different groups and individuals will need different strategies for influencing. It will be very important to customize your influencing tactic for each person, with individual personalities, goals, and objectives, including organizational roles and responsibilities, in mind.

✔ **Assess the Situation.** The fundamental questions that you should first ask yourself are: *Why am I involved in this work area? Why am I in need of this other person's input? What kind of results am I trying to achieve by influencing this person?* One of the most important things to remember in this category is that you should be very clear about whom you need to influence and your set targets.

✔ **Review Your Ability.** Which tactics do you use occasionally? Which ones are most effective when used? Are there any new tactics that could be used in this situation? Can you also be inspired by others for advice or coaching? For example, if you are always focusing on making logical appeals to colleagues, then it is prudent that you have a co-worker who is a very dedicated collaborator to help you put forth your collaboration tactics and arguments.

✔ **Brainstorm Your Approach.** What are the tactics that best work for you? Which logical appeals do you think are most effective when used? How do you make either an emotional or a cooperative appeal? What exactly would you say or do in each tactic? You need to anticipate possible responses so that you adequately prepare your reply. Do you have any counterarguments that you could use? Are there any additional influencing tactics to help you through?

When starting out as a leader or in a management position, at first, it would be vital for you to try out new influencing tactics in low-risk situations, by practicing one-on-one. Then as you grow more versatile and experienced, you will gain enough confidence in your abilities in influencing other teams and larger groups. Through this experience, you will be able to persuade others in higher-stakes situations easily.

Find the approach that works best for you.

Grow Your Core Leadership Skills for Every Role

To be effective as a leader, there is a great need for you to continue developing, adapting, and strengthening your skills throughout your career. As you also gain skill in one area, you will find that there is more to be learned and practiced when moving on to new challenges and frontiers, taking on larger roles. If, as a leader, you feel that you have skipped any of the above fundamental core leadership skills in your career, then there is no need to feel inadequate that you will not be as effective as you want or that you can't fully develop your leadership skills. On the contrary, with concerted effort, you can always learn and improve skills that you missed out on. Moreover, if you can identify gaps or weaknesses in your leadership skills, then this positive mentality will enable you to have the potential to learn, grow, and change for the better. Thus, through self-awareness, communication, influence, and learning agility as the core of your leadership development and values, you can rest assured that you are setting yourself up for new opportunities and into new levels of responsibility, this is because these four core leadership skills are needed for everyone and in every stage of your career.

Dale Carnegie, in his book called *How to Win Friends and Influence People*, describes how to influence others positively and maintain great friendship as a result. Even though this book was written in 1936, these principles and lessons have stood the test of time and are always a point of reference for many influential leaders today. What stands out about these principles is that they are not about trends or fads, but are the building blocks of social intelligence, and how the practice of good social skills can improve your life.

Below are the ten best classic lessons and principles we learn from Carnegie:

1. Do Not Criticize, Condemn, or Complain

A quote from the book says, "Any fool can criticize, condemn or complain—and most fools do." Carnegie goes on to say that it takes great amounts of character and self-control to forgive for the wrongs done to you. This discipline will bring you great dividends and joy in the manner in which you relate to other people.

2. Be Generous with Praise

Carnegie recommends using praise generously in relationships, quoting Charles M. Schwab, who said:

> "In my wide association in life, meeting with many and great people in various parts of the world, I am yet to find the person, however great or exalted in their station, who did not do better work and put forth greater effort under a spirit of approval than they would ever do under a spirit of criticism."

3. Remember People's Names

It is very difficult at times to remember people's names when you meet them for the first time, especially when you meet many people casually. However, it is possible if you train yourself in remembering names. This will make people feel very special, appreciated, and important. Carnegie goes on to say that, "Remember that a person's name is the most important and sweetest sound in any language."

4. Be Genuinely Interested in Others

Remembering people's names, and asking them questions, which will encourage them to talk freely about themselves and their interests, will eventually make people believe that you like them. They will, in turn, like you. Carnegie continues to write. "You can make more friends in two months by becoming interested in other people than you can in two years by trying to get other people interested in you." It is important for you to listen 75% and only speak 25% at all times.

5. Know the Value of Charm

People normally do not discuss the fact that when it comes to looking for jobs, getting an opportunity is not about talent, which college you attended, or who do you know, it is all about people liking you. A good resume may get you an interview, but it is your charisma, social skills, and talent that will make people want to keep you around. This is the reason why people will always pick someone whom they enjoy being around over someone they don't, no matter how talented he/she is. This has the potential to enrich your life and will, in turn, open as many doors as you ever imagined possible.

6. Be Quick to Acknowledge Your Own Mistakes

Humility beats all else. It softens even the hardest of hearts. Being humble will make people less defensive and more agreeable than when you are humble and reasonable at the same time but not enough to take responsibility for your own mistakes. It is very important to have a strong and stable personal and professional relationship with others. This will greatly hinge on you being responsible for your actions, especially when it comes to your mistakes.

7. Don't Attempt to "Win" an Argument

Carnegie writes that the best manner to win an argument is to avoid it, citing the adage: "A man convinced against his will, will still have the same opinion." Even if you can completely dismantle the other party's argument with factual information, it will not change their mind.

8. Begin on Common Ground

In the event of a disagreement, it is very prudent for both of you to start on common ground, which will make it very easy for the two of you to transition into the difficult subjects. If you start from polarizing positions, you stand to lose in a big way and might never recover lost ground even on the subjects that you originally agreed upon.

9. Have Others Believe Your Conclusion Is Their Own

You cannot force people to believe anything that they are told. This is why those people who are persuasive greatly understand how suggestion has tremendous power. You need to learn how to plant a seed, instead of telling people they are wrong, and look for common ground, so you can then easily persuade them that what they want is actually your (unspoken) desired outcome.

10. Make People Feel Important

You can achieve this without much effort: it does not cost you anything to smile; know people's names; praise them; and make an effort to learn their interests and really listen to them when they talk. All of these details can make people feel important.

Hack Others' Mind with Cognitive Biases

We human beings tend to believe that we are rational and logical in our undertakings. However, unbeknown to us, we are constantly under the influence of cognitive biases that influence our thinking, beliefs, and every other decision and judgment that we make daily.

At times, these biases can be very obvious to the discerning, and one might even recognize these predispositions while they are so hidden that they are not easy to notice.

Below are some of these cognitive biases that have a profound influence on the way we live our daily lives:

The Confirmation Bias

This type of bias is based on how people tend to listen more to information that reaffirms what they already know or believe.

The Hindsight Bias

This type of bias involves the tendency to see previous events, whether random or not, as being more predictable than they actually were.

The Anchoring Bias

As human beings, we always tend to gravitate toward the first piece of information that we receive. This is what is called the anchoring bias or anchoring effect.

The Misinformation Effect

We can be greatly influenced by memories of particular events in our lives. This involves conflating things that actually occurred after a specific event, as having occurred during the event itself. This is what we refer to as the misinformation effect.

The False-Consensus Effect

People tend to overestimate how much other people might agree with their own beliefs, behaviors, attitudes, and values. Thus, this inclination is what is known as the false consensus effect. This can, at times, make a person overvalue their views.

What is the Barnum Effect?

The "Barnum Effect" is also known as the "Forer Effect" in the field of psychology. It is a phenomenon that tends to occur when people believe that general descriptions of personalities are applied specifically to them. Therefore, this effect means that people can be gullible, due to their thinking that information is about them only, when really it is generic. The name of this effect was inspired by the phrase "There's a sucker born every minute," which has mostly been attributed to showman P.T. Barnum (though there is no evidence that he said it).

What is a "Barnum" statement?

How to Use Barnum Statements to Influence People

Astrologists, who use horoscopes, magicians, palm readers, and psychics gazing at crystal balls, make extensive use of the Barnum Effect, by convincing people that their often generic descriptions of them are highly specialized and unique; hence, they cannot apply to anyone else.

Barnum Statements are positive statements that most people will agree on, in regard to themselves. They might not be aware that almost every other person will also see themselves in the statements, and they are not, in fact, personalized.

PART 3: Unlocking Your Powers

Chapter 12: NLP: Master Persuasion & Negotiation Techniques

There is a strong relationship between Neuro-Linguistic Programming (NLP) and persuasion and influence. For starters, Neuro-Linguistic Programming involves studying the subjective human experience. It involves studying how people can create some meaning within the mind. According to some individuals, Neuro-Linguistic Programming involves studying superior thinking. Human beings usually create a sense of meaning both externally and internally. It is also possible to learn more about how people express themselves through spoken language and how they can be influenced. Language can be used to persuade people and it is an instrument that can be used to transmit internal experiences.

State Control

When it comes to influencing and persuading people, the first thing that you need to consider is whether you have a close relationship with the person. If a personal relationship does not exist, it would be difficult to persuade or influence someone. On the other hand, it is possible to create a personal relationship with someone using Neuro-Linguistic Programming. "State control" should always come about before you can focus on ensuring that you have developed a personal relationship.

NLP also allows you to learn more about how you can control your state. If you can form a close relationship with someone and observe how you feel when they are in a bad mood, for example, you should be able to gauge the feeling that you have. There are some instances whereby people feel energetic. State control is defined as the ability to link various sequences of emotional states at any given moment. It is possible to learn these techniques through Neuro-Linguistic Programming.

It is also good to note that if you are not in the right state, you cannot easily form a close relationship with someone, regardless of whether you have an in-depth understanding of Neuro-Linguistic Programming. When forming a close relationship with a person, you should ensure that your psycho-emotional state matches that of the other party. After studying Neuro-Linguistic Programming, you will be able to learn various mechanical techniques including;

> Using the verbs being used by other parties.
> Being able to match breathing patterns.
> Using the tonalities used by the other party.
> Matching their way of blinking.
> Using the posture they normally use.

After learning about Neuro-Linguistic Programming, it is possible to take your own physiology and to make sure that it matches that of the other person. It is also good to note that a close relationship cannot be formed if you are not close to the other person. The main point to note is that the NLP techniques allow people to speed up the process of becoming close to someone, while also ensuring that their frequency aligns with that of the other person, within a short period.

Classical Neuro-Linguistic Programming allows you to assume the character of the other party easily and fully, and you can easily persuade and influence them. It is also possible to fully mimic the individual. Such an eventuality is known as "pacing." Pacing involves imitating someone or talking about some things that may be true, depending on a specific experience.

You may want to form a close relationship with someone who is in a negative state, and you may not know how to go about it. If you want to form a bond with a person who is in a negative state, you won't want to be in the same negative state as them. Such consideration comes about since you must be in the same state as the other person you want to form a rapport with. Some of the phenomena that comes into play includes the presence of mirror neurons; these neurons can help you to form a desired connection with the other party.

It is also possible to change someone's state. When approaching someone, you must first observe the environment. You may have different options, and they include interrupting the other person. Most people lack the courage to interrupt a person. The other option involves ensuring that you can match the other person's state. By changing their state to your own, you can easily change the state of the other individual.

When you approach a person and depict high energy levels, there might be a huge difference in the frequency of the two parties, and you may fail to relate. For instance, your energy levels may be higher than that of the target individual, and that means that your states cannot align. Also, some states cannot be easily interrupted. The moment when you form a connection with someone and your frequencies do not align, it is still possible that you will relate.

What are the Fundamentals of Human Behavior and Change?

Events such as modeling, action, and effective communication are some of the key components of Neuro-Linguistic Programming. The belief here is that if an individual can understand how the other party accomplishes a task, then the overall process can easily be copied and communicated to others at the same time for them to also complete the task at hand.

Proponents of this concept opine that everyone has a personal map of reality. Therefore, those who practice NLP normally analyze their own idea of reality, and any other perspectives, to come up with a workable and systematic overview of a situation. By understanding a wide range of perspectives, these NLP users gain considerable amounts of information. Those advocating for this concept believe that our senses play a vital role when it comes to processing the available information and that our bodies and mind can influence one another. Hence, Neuro-Linguistic Programming is an experiential approach to all this, and for anyone to understand an action, then surely they must perform that same action if they are to learn from the experience.

Moreover, NLP practitioners have this belief that there are natural hierarchies when it comes to learning, communicating, and change. The six logical levels of change are listed below:

> **Spirituality and Purpose** - this can be termed as involvement in something that might be larger than life. It could be involvement in matters of religion, ethics, or any other system. This presents one of the highest levels of change.

> **Identity** - this normally involves how you view yourself. It can also include the responsibilities and other roles in your life.

> **Beliefs and Values** - This system entails all your personal beliefs, including all the issues that matter in every aspect of your life.

Capabilities and Skills - This category involves all your abilities and what you can accomplish by using them.

Behaviors - These are the specific actions, which you can perform.

Environment - This is your setting, including where you live. It also includes the people around you. Normally, this is seen as the lowest level of change one can effect.

The purpose of each of these logical levels in our lives is to organize and direct any flow of information. Therefore, when it comes to making any change in the lower tier, it can also have an overall effect on the higher levels. The same theory also applies to changes in the higher levels, according to NLP practitioners.

How to Safeguard Yourself from Manipulation/Persuasion

All our emotions, whether good or bad, have a certain purpose in our lives. However, you should be on the lookout for those who want to exploit you for their own personal gains by using the mighty power of emotions. Any time you feel emotionally drained, it is important for you to go through these tips below for the protection of your very own energy field against external exploitation.

1. Don't Fall into Their Trap

In this world, some people take great pleasure in exploiting other people's emotions and will use every trick in the book to their advantage. These are elements that include confusion, blame games, and interrogation, to get the better of you. You need to find ways of effectively dealing with them. You can achieve this by ignoring them or politely refusing their advances, as opposed to meeting them.

2. Start Writing Down What They Say During Conversations

While this might be a bit awkward, emotional manipulators tend to make you look bad. The trick is to twist their words to fit their motive. If you are not careful, you may even start to take their word for it and believe what they say. To ensure that it does not happen, you can replay the things they said in previous conversations by writing down every detail you might feel is important in countering them.

3. Steer Clear Whenever Possible

Just steer clear of these types of people. This is because emotional manipulators are very clever people who will stop at nothing to take advantage of you and will render slim any chance of you taking advantage of them.

4. Call Them out on Their Behavior

These people know how the human mind works, simply because they have probably been able to boss people around and they have never been caught out or held accountable for their actions. Therefore, when confronted by these con artists, you must stand up for yourself. Let it be known that you do not condone any form of nonsense from them.

5. Avoid Emotional Attachment with Them

I know this might be easier said than done. This is especially so when they do not initially show their true identity. However, as a potential victim, you should pay close attention to the first signs that might indicate they are about to open up your emotional roller coaster. Slowly but surely, back away from this toxic relationship for your own benefit. Make sure that you make them know your boundaries. One thing that emotional manipulators are good at is that they are constantly on the lookout for their next prey. However, it would be easier for you to break away if you have not invested much emotionally in this relationship.

6. Meditate Often

For you not to be caught off-guard, you must always keep a positive mindset through constant meditation, by keeping your mind silent, deep breaths, if possible get in touch with the higher realms to adequately handle yourself down here on Earth. This will come in handy when dealing with emotional manipulators, in the best manner possible. This is because you are assured of inner peace no matter the amount of chaos that surrounds you; you will have great composure within yourself. Meditations of love and kindness will enable you to look at such a person in a different light, enabling you to develop compassion for them. It may even open your eyes to see the possibilities of what they have gone through in their lives for them to be the way they are. You will always have peace of mind when you practice the art of meeting hostility with love and understanding. You never know that it is such gestures that may transform an emotional manipulator into a new being after all.

7. Inspire Them

In this regard, you need to be the agent of change. This will position you at a great advantage because it will inadvertently shield you from any negative sentiments that may be thrown at you by emotional manipulators after your own non-manipulative and positive countermeasures have inspired them. If need be, to stall them in their tracks, bring out the benefits that come with meditating, and the simple ways in which they can take responsibility for their own actions and lives, among other life's positive attributes.

8. Tell Them, "You're Right"

As hard as it might seem for your ego, you will always have peace of mind, and your soul will always rest easy knowing that you are composed and cannot be taken advantage of by these parasites. Emotional manipulators always thrive on drama, and the better if you agree with them on anything they say. This, in turn, will leave them clueless, quickly extinguishing any hope that they had of exploiting your emotions. This is because, for the sake of your emotional wellbeing and peace of mind, you just let them have their way in the argument. However, deep within yourself, you darn well know that everything being said about you is false.

9. Let Go of Harmful Relationships

If you realize that either your boyfriend or girlfriend has the tendency to be emotionally manipulative, then the best thing for you is to leave the relationship early enough while your dignity and self-worth are still high. This is for your own good and peace of mind. You can never impose change on anyone who is like this, no matter the countless times that you have brought forth their violent behavior or put up with them. Someone of your caliber deserves someone who will nurture and take good care of you and your emotional well-being, and not someone who wants to take advantage of you for their own selfish motives.

10. Develop a Strong Mentality

You should never let another person's insults and outbursts get the better of you. Remember, this is just a ploy to get under your skin. Instead, the best thing you could do for yourself is to find humor in these insults. Another trick you could do is entertaining their sentiments without seemingly agreeing with them. If you have an unshakable and strong sense of self-esteem, then nothing they say will get into your head.

11. Give Yourself Positive Self-Talk Throughout the Day

Masters of emotional manipulation can destroy your image and mood. Ensure that you can restore everything by uplifting yourself to greater heights where nobody can pluck them. This is because they thrive best when they see you battered and bruised emotionally. That is when they swoop in for the kill. However, when they see that you are unperturbed by their advances, they will leave you alone; hence, they will not have any valid reason to get closer to you any longer.

Some other suitable negotiation techniques:

Frame the Negotiation as a Collaboration, and it Will Be Used to Solve a Common Problem

The most important factor to note is that the main focus should be on the opponent since they are the main problem. You should not come up with a "me" vs. "them" mentality. Also, your choice of words and body language should not showcase that you are bringing about some competitiveness. The first step should entail establishing your goals. After you come up with your objectives, you can work with a more general purpose.

No Immediate Retort

This is an important skill that you should possess so that you can handle a negotiation effectively. After a person comes up with an idea, you should not come up with a counter-argument immediately. First, share the ideas that you have. After that, the person who came up with the idea will be more interested in hearing what you have to say. Do not try to pin your idea fast. Ensure that you have discussed the initial idea accordingly. You can also come up with some questions and explore the proposal that has been brought forth. After some time, the other party will start to address any concerns that you may have.

Chapter 13: The Antidote to Groupthink: 10 Ways to Beat the Herd

Groupthink – this is a term used to describe what takes place when a group of people comes together, and their main desire is to maintain harmony within the group at any cost. The desire to maintain cohesiveness brings about a tendency whereby all the members come to a consensus without arguing at all, even if this is irrational or damaging to the project. There will be minimal conflict but also a lack of creativity and critical thinking; the main issue is that people will come to a conclusion before even evaluating their decision effectively.

After learning about what Groupthink entails, we will now look into ten ways through which you can beat the herd. Some tips from the experts include:

1. Plan for Everything

If a risky plan is being discussed, it is advisable to come up with plans for all conceivable scenarios. It does not mean that the group will fail; however, it is good to start by tackling the underlying problem as it is, rather than ignoring it.

2. Encouraging a Debate

When you get your way through a debate, you will feel good; however, the feeling will be short-lived, and the end result may also not be desirable. As a leader within a team, you should be bold enough to face the team members and emphasize how different ideas should be discussed further. People can also express their opinions while also challenging the opinions put across by others. For instance, in business, happy-talk may be common; however, there should be another discussion that will ensure that people get to learn more about different business endeavors. The main focus here is on increasing your knowledge base. By doing so, you will be able to overcome Groupthink.

3. Looking for Different Personalities

In a group, the majority of the members should possess different personalities. Some of these personalities include the presence of a creative problem solver, an unorthodox thinker, a person who works well under pressure, and the person who judges the opinions that have been put across by other members of the group. The judgment should be made in an objective manner. Make sure that you have looked for people who have varying styles of communicating and thinking.

4. Acknowledge the Bias in the Data

Some leaders may assume that by relying on data, they may eliminate Groupthink. At times, an analyst may not issue accurate information, and they may pick different pieces of information in a bid to please the managers. Based on this inaccurate information, the managers may be reassured about the decisions that they have implemented, and they may fail to make improvements. After some of the misleading insights are approved, they may be harder to challenge. As a leader, you should make sure that you have not revealed your "hopes and dreams" to a data scientist that you have hired to mine and collect some information, as this might influence the report.

5. Reaching Out

Always invite people from other departments, especially if they have been affected by some of the decisions that you have made. Even if the invited people fail to attend the meeting, make an effort to reach out to other people within the company, and they should issue some feedback. People within an organization should avoid being influenced by the ideas within the group, and they may be willing to offer independent ideas and options.

6. Understand that Speed Can Kill

At times, when people reach a decision quickly, the group may be relieved. Speed can indeed kill, and that is why a group should not make a decision hastily. First, everyone should issue their own opinion. If a leader believes that the debate was not enough, they should delay the decision and make sure that the other group members have carried out further research.

7. Increasing Awareness

As a leader, you should focus on ensuring that you have created awareness within the group in a bid to prevent Groupthink. The leader should ensure that people are aware of what Groupthink is and how it takes place. Also, they should be informed about the consequences of Groupthink.

8. Take Part in Open Discussions

While in a group, it is advisable to create a culture whereby the employees will be encouraged to analyze the situations accordingly while issuing feedback and sharing information.

9. You Should Not Shoot the Messenger

When engaging in an open discussion, you should avoid a lot of criticism. At times, when a person comes up with an alternative opinion, they may be criticized by the other members. People within a group should learn more about critical listening skills.

10. Assign the "Devil's Advocate"

As a leader, you should consult one or two members and ask them whether they would be comfortable playing the role of the devil's advocate. The group should be divided twice, and one team should look into the pros, whereas the other team should focus on the cons of a certain opinion.

We have looked into ten ways through which Groupthink can be eliminated. There are also other ways through which Groupthink can be eliminated, and they include:

- **Consulting Some of the Subject Matter Experts**

When discussing a very important topic, some subject matters may be involved, and they may be present in the group. In some instances, the group may have to hire a subject expert externally. A subject expert is a person who understands everything about a certain subject, and they can offer some insight into the present consequences associated with a specific opinion. Also, they can look into some of the present alternatives that will be suitable in each case.

- **The Decisions Should Be Documented**

After the group has reached a decision, the members can go ahead and document the information.

- Some of the possible solutions and each option should be analyzed thoroughly.

- The present situation and some of the associated issues.

- The recommended solution and why it is preferable.

- A plan that is implementable. The budget and the timeline should also be presented.

- **A Group May Ask for an Opinion from Another Team**

At times, some of the group members may not be comfortable with the decisions that they have made, and they may solicit some opinions from another team. The other team will review the provided document, and give feedback.

Finally, it is good to note that when collaborating as group members at the workplace, the learners should sit back as a way of avoiding Groupthink and the presence of ideas that lack a touch of creativity. If one of the leaders can make good use of the creativity demonstrated by one of the group members, they can channel it accordingly, and they may produce a more desirable outcome.

Chapter 14: Body Language: Speed-Reading and Sending out the Right Message

Perhaps you have been wondering how life would be if someone could read another person's mind. Some people know how to make good use of their intuition for such issues. But others are not exactly good at it. For people who cannot use their perception, there is one ideal option left. It is learning how to study a person's body language. That said, it is a fact that people can get up to 45 percent of information from nonverbal communication. Experts specializing in body language have written in the past that people can often study the gestures as well as other additional body movements of an individual to unmask the character of a person and then tell what they think or, better yet, feel. Mimics can also be used to analyze a person's character. Other professionals have added that you should pay attention to various signals sent by other people without them realizing it. While most people may not consider narcissism as well as psychopathy desirable traits in friends as well as lovers, most of us are strangely drawn toward people with the mentioned personality traits. As such, "mean girls" are usually popularly known in school.

Vampires are known to be sex symbols. But in recent research, it was concluded that people commonly referred to as individuals with dark personalities are physically attractive compared to others. So, what is it really about these dark personalities that make these individuals as appealing as stated in the research studies? What makes them tick? Why do people fall into their trap? The answers to these questions can assist us in comprehending what makes individuals with such personalities successful when it comes to exploiting other people.

To test that, two professionals are known as Nicholas Holtzman, as well as Michael Strube of the prestigious Washington University, studied the relationship between people's tendencies and their attractive nature. They also analyzed the relationship between people and psychopathy, in addition to Machiavellianism. These researchers wanted to determine whether the traits mentioned, which are also referred to as the Dark Triad, are directly linked with the ability to enhance a person's physical appearance. To test the idea, these professionals decided to invite up to 100 students into a laboratory. Every student was asked to take a photograph immediately. After that, every student was asked to put on a grey pair of pants and a shirt. The women in the team were asked to cleanse their faces by removing makeup. Individuals with long hair were asked to wear their hair into a ponytail. The students were photographed.

The two professionals took the two sets of photographs and compared them. This was in terms of their physical appearance. They were in a position to determine their looks, including how attractive every student was. The professionals assessed these candidate's personalities, including their tendencies towards psychopathy. Candidates were asked to rate themselves and then share their friend's contact details. It was decided that their friends should leave ratings too. The combination of peer ratings was then used in calculating the set of various personality scores for students. The ratings provided by students based on narcissism and psychopathy were also merged to create a major composite known as the Dark Triad.

The Dark Triad was pretty much correlated with the attractive candidates. But, the score of the Dark Triad was not primarily related to the physical attractiveness of the candidates once they were stripped down to basic clothes and hair. People who had a dark personality trait were not seen as physically attractive compared to others, especially when you take away their freedom when it comes to wearing their clothes as well as makeup. People who had dark personalities were good at dressing up. Following a detailed introduction, it was concluded that every student should fill out a survey that asked their opinion regarding first impressions. The candidates who scored high marks when it comes to narcissism were likable. These findings have reinforced initial research indicating narcissists are more well known and liked than others, at least at first.

Candidates seen as likable were more narcissistic with flashier appearances and confident body language. Researchers concluded that narcissists are good at carrying as well as presenting themselves in such a way that they can easily impress others instantly. This is also an additional reason why it is crucial to take time to judge a person's character when meeting for the first time. The first step of resisting a person with a Dark Triad trait is not easy. If they are physically attractive,s this is also automatically attached to other positive traits, in the "halo effect." When someone is perceived as physically attractive, we may assume that they are kind in nature as well as more confident. To create an advantageous environment, the person needs to look attractive physically. When a person's physical attractiveness merges with their confidence they are more effective when it comes to deceiving someone. It also appears that individuals with exploitive personalities are relatively more successful at this.

Analyzing Different Body Language

You may feel that you comprehend all the manipulation tactics, including how to use them to, win the hearts of your peers or family. However, it is still important to garner more information regarding body language and how you can persuade various people around you. While there are several differences in people, there are also a couple of similarities. To better analyze people around you, you need to find a few elements that can help you to connect with them by bringing you together rather than tearing you apart. It is also important to note that manipulation is a negative trait. We, therefore, emphasize the need to understand how to read body language. In this chapter, we shall look at some of the main body language cues involved in the Dark Triad and teach you how to analyze them:

Closing the Eyes

If the person you are talking with closes their eyes, then they are on the verge of telling a lie. You need to remember that it does not imply they are scared of you. Rather, it means that they are evasive because they do not want to deal with the situation at hand. They could also be trying to avoid you.

Presenting the Face

This is a gesture used to attract individuals of the opposite sex. When a person places their chin on the hands, they present their face to be viewed as if trying to say "This is me." Therefore, you are often allowed to enjoy what you are seeing. For men, it is important to memorize this kind of gesture to be in a position to catch a complimentary moment.

Arms on The Chest

The next body language we shall look into is the arms crossed over a person's chest. This is an ideal example of defensive individuals. It is often used to demonstrate that a person disagrees with certain opinions as well as the actions of others regardless of their relationship.

Touching the Nose

When an individual touches their nose when talking, it can always signify a couple of things. First, it could be rejection. Then secondly, it could be a way of demonstrating a person's dishonesty when it comes to what they are saying.

Palms Open

When a person opens their palms facing upward, it could be a symbol of being honest or open to a stated idea. That said, in older centuries, when individuals carried their weapons, the sign was used to indicate that they were armless and sincere. Over the years, it became a consistent practice indicative of innocence. When a person puts head in hands, it is an ideal example of a body language that could imply the individual is upset. Therefore, they may not be interested in showing their face. Locked ankles indicate that a person is nervous.

Rubbing the Chin

The chin is often rubbed when someone is trying to make a crucial yet viable decision. The person could be looking down or sideways. But they hardly know exactly what they want since they are thinking critically and deeply. The throat below the chin is also vulnerable, therefore, a predator can easily use it to attack an individual. Holding the chin is a protective measure for the throat. It is also one of the ways through which people act defensively. Holding the chin is also a symbol of being submissive.

Sending Out the Right Message

Without a doubt, it is vital to learn how to communicate nonverbally. This is usually in the form of someone's body language. The method has a significant impact on how the message is communicated and then received by other people. Nonverbal communication is also vital in business. Workplace communication drives various activities between customers and service providers.

Give these tips a try:

Watch Out for Yourself and Others

When in the process of communicating with other people, you should be attentive to the type of messages you intend to send via your body. Do your words match the nonverbal language? In case they do not, then it is time to fix them. That said, people are often gifted with the knowledge to grasp the nonverbal cues.

Remember to Maintain Eye Contact

It is crucial to maintain eye contact, especially when talking with other people, such as coworkers and employers. With eye contact, you shall be building trust. At the same time, you will be able to use eye contact to send a relatively strong message to other people if you are not comfortable.

Chapter 15: Creating your OWN Thoughts

We are often told to guard our thoughts since they tend to influence our actions, and that our thoughts have power.

But we rarely look at the origins of our thoughts, since we may not necessarily like what we find; some of us may discover that our thoughts are influenced unconsciously by trauma, fear, lack of knowledge on a particular subject, or maybe we have even been influenced or manipulated by a friend or partner.

How many times have you seen an Instagram post showcasing the latest fashions and thought to yourself, "I must have that." Or when you were enjoying some screen-time and a marketing ad for a new product, you immediately thought "I must have that too."

What of Groupthink? I guarantee most of us may have fallen victim to this one and have been part of a group. Not all outside influence is bad; as a matter of fact, some can be very instrumental in ensuring we come to the right conclusions. However, at times when engaging in Groupthink we may feel too afraid to voice our individual thoughts that differ from the group. There are various options or alternatives to discuss but this chapter will focus on one solution without serious deliberations.

So how does one go about the process of creating their own thoughts without any influences? Well here are some tips to create your own thoughts:

1. Creating Your Own Identity

This involves creating one's own sense of self. That means clearly defining your interests and preferences. Having a clear picture of who exactly you are, what you love to wear, and how you would love to look. This will help you not to fall victim to influence from media ads that tell you what you should wear, what products you should use, or how you should look.

2. Acquiring Adequate Knowledge

One should aim at having adequate knowledge about a subject or situation before forming an opinion. You should learn to constantly obtain knowledge either from reading books, observing situations, and listening keenly before coming to a conclusion.

For example, this can help so you aren't influenced to purchase a product or service which you may not be fully aware of.

3. Learning to Be Flexible

You should not imagine that only specific solutions will work for specific problems, sometimes they might. But if they don't, always be open to discover other solutions to the problem, weigh in on their pros and cons and try to see if they could work. And before you say "no," also aim to look at each solution from all different perspectives, then see if they have any negative consequences and if they harm anyone. If they don't, then try to implement them or factor them in as possible solutions.

4. Learning to Point out Possible Biases

We can often find it hard to judge a situation for what it is, as we often unconsciously factor in our cultural biases or our own upbringing and other people's opinion. Therefore, we end up deciding from a wrong perspective. Try to take the time to evaluate the situation without any biases, observe things first-hand, and then form very clear opinions about the subject or situation.

5. Not Caving in to Fear, Pressure and Guilt

Sometimes we may find it hard to voice our opinions if they differ from the group's, as we may fear that it will cause disagreements or for us to have labels. However, it is important to stand by your opinions regardless, since sometimes it may be the right thing to do. Other times it may just be the brilliant idea that everyone has been waiting to hear, furthermore, in a healthy argument, it is important to have everyone's opinion before you come to any conclusions.

Benefits of Creating Your Own Thoughts

While you may be enjoying your newfound power to create your own thoughts and opinions without any hindrances, here are some of the other benefits you may receive:

1. You tend to become more interesting to others since every time they have conversations with you, you challenge their opinions and thoughts.

2. You are constantly self-improving since you are always trying to seek different perspectives toward different situations. And you are always looking for different alternative situations to different problems.

3. You become more alert toward any persuasion or influence from the media.

4. You tend to gain respect from the people around you as they value your opinions since they are always original. They also value the fact that you are constantly standing up for them.

5. Your mind and mind power are always developing.

6. You develop trust in yourself and your abilities and therefore end up having great self-confidence.

Tips to Identify That You May Not Be Creating Your Own Thoughts

While creating your own thoughts can be quite essential and beneficial, sometimes, you may find yourself taking a few steps back. When you do, here are some of the tips that can let you know that you aren't thinking for yourself:

1. You may not take the time to evaluate things or situations before forming opinions on them.

2. You may find yourself doing some things the same way since they have always been done that way.

3. You may slowly find yourself buying into stereotypes based on sex, race, or culture.

4. You may find yourself being easily swayed by the media, another person, or a group of people.

Creating your own thoughts is very important as you get to form very clear opinions that help you in making very insightful decisions.

Conclusion

I hope you enjoyed reading *Dark Psychology: Master Persuasion, Negotiation and NLP and Unlock the Power of Understanding Manipulation, Deception, Mind Control, Human Behavior, Psychological Warfare, and Brainwashing.* I also hope that this Dark Psychology handbook was informative when it comes to learning more about Neuro-Linguistic Programming (NLP), master persuasion, and psychology, with regard to how people are manipulated and how to avoid manipulation.

The book has also been published with the sole aim of impacting people's lives positively. Always remember that you should focus on the chapters that discuss more about the strategies used by manipulative people and how you can avoid becoming a victim. After all, no one likes being manipulated by another person. I bet that you do not want to be associated with manipulative people, and some of the strategies that have been highlighted in this book will ensure that you can navigate your way out of some tricky situations.

Finally, if you found this book useful in any way, a review on Amazon is always appreciated!

Sources

https://www.darkpsychology.co/dark-psychology/

https://www.youtube.com/watch?v=UAIEvoz_RJA

https://www.psychologytoday.com/intl/blog/toxic-relationships/201812/how-spot-narcissist

https://psychcentral.com/lib/how-to-recognize-a-psychopath/

https://www.spring.org.uk/2018/08/machiavellian-personality-disorder.php

https://www.psychologytoday.com/intl/blog/sex-murder-and-the-meaning-life/201412/the-four-dark-personality-traits

https://www.youtube.com/watch?v=JuhqwEf8kSY

https://www.apa.org/monitor/2014/02/criminal-mind

https://online.maryville.edu/online-bachelors-degrees/forensic-psychology/historys-famous-crooks/

https://www.darkpsychology.co/cybercriminal-minds/https://www.effective-living.com/3290/warning-signs-of-a-criminal-mind/

https://openpsychometrics.org/tests/SD3/

https://www.youtube.com/watch?v=sUCG3osf4lA

https://www.youtube.com/watch?v=qL33TRP7qiE

https://www.cracked.com/article_19646_5-creepy-forms-mind-control-youre-exposed-to-daily.html

https://interestingengineering.com/the-cias-mind-control-and-lsd-program-mk-ultra

https://www.psychologytoday.com/us/basics/deception

https://www.fraud-magazine.com/article.aspx?id=4294971184

https://www.youtube.com/watch?v=P_6vDLq64gE&t=63s ,

https://www.inc.com/justin-bariso/an-fbi-agent-s-8-ways-to-spot-a-liar.html

https://www.thehealthy.com/family/relationships/how-to-spot-a-liar/

https://www.theguardian.com/commentisfree/belief/2009/may/27/cults-definition-religion

http://cultresearch.org/help/characteristics-associated-with-cults/

https://psychcentral.com/blog/media-manipulation-of-the-masses-how-the-media-psychologically-manipulates/

https://exploringyourmind.com/10-strategies-of-media-manipulation/

https://newseumed.org/cantdupeme

https://www.wvik.org/post/why-political-propaganda-works-and-how-spot-it

https://www.historians.org/about-aha-and-membership/aha-history-and-archives/gi-roundtable-series/pamphlets/em-2-what-is-propaganda-(1944)/what-are-the-tools-of-propaganda

https://spectrum.ieee.org/computing/software/how-political-campaigns-weaponize-social-media-bots

https://study.com/academy/lesson/what-is-psychological-warfare-definition-techniques-examples.html

https://medium.com/@womanistpsych/psychological-warfare-tactics-manipulating-your-vote-182d754961cd

https://www.listeningpartnership.com/insight/master-manipulator/

https://inlpcenter.org/what-is-neuro-linguistic-programming-nlp/

https://www.the-secret-of-mindpower-and-nlp.com/NLP-techniques-for-persuasion.html

https://happyrubin.com/nlp/negotiation/

https://theplaidzebra.com/the-6-nlp-techniques-that-will-turn-you-into-an-expert-negotiator/

https://www.verywellmind.com/what-is-groupthink-2795213

https://highfive.com/blog/8-steps-to-avoid-groupthink

https://www.youtube.com/watch?v=4jwUXV4QaTw

https://www.insider.com/subtle-signs-that-youre-talking-to-a-psychopath-2018-2

https://www.businessinsider.com/how-to-tell-if-you-are-talking-to-a-psychopath-or-narcissist-2017-12#psychopaths-tend-to-use-emotional-language-without-displaying-much-feeling-3

https://www.huffingtonpost.co.uk/dr-raj-persaud/dont-walk-this-way-how-yo_b_6509478.html

https://www.inc.com/amy-morin/advice-from-a-therapist-5-ways-to-with-a-psychopath-at-work.html

https://www.iflscience.com/brain/manipulative-psychopaths-lose-their-mischievous-powers-when-talking-online/

https://www.essentiallifeskills.net/think-for-yourself.html

https://www.aconsciousrethink.com/8349/thinking-for-yourself/

Printed in Great Britain
by Amazon